On a magnificent clear day, a hiker makes his way through a section of dense, ridgetop vegetation on the Koʻolau Crest Trail near Poamoho.

Adventurer's Hawai'i

Photographic Glimpses of the Hawaiian Islands as seen by the Hiker, Kayaker, and Adventurer.

by Peter Caldwell

Taote Publishing
Honolulu, Hawai'i

Taote Publishing
P.O. Box 22660
Honolulu, Hawaii 96823

Photographs by the author.

Design by Lynne Meyer, LM Graphics.

Printed in Singapore by Toppan.

Publishers Cataloging in Publication Data.

Library of Congress Catalog Card #92-080609.

ISBN 0-9626124-1-3

Author's Note

The scenic wonders of Hawai'i have been well documented in numerous magazines, articles, and books. Memorable, familiar landmarks such as Waimea Canyon on Kaua'i, Maui's Haleakalā Crater, and the Big Island's 'Akaka Falls have been beautifully photographed many times. However, there is much more to be found in the Hawaiian Islands than the usual images featured in glossy tourist brochures and coffee-table publications.

The majority of these areas are accessible only to the hiker, kayaker, and adventurer. There is always a tendency to hesitate when considering anything that will draw attention to such special places. Would it not be better to safeguard them by not sharing their secrets? Nevertheless, with more knowledge about the unique and unspoiled areas that still remain in our island environment, hopefully there will be more incentive to preserve and protect them for future generations. This book is not meant to be a guide with specific information about trails, routes, and access. Individuals interested in visiting these places can obtain more details from the sources listed in the appendix.

This collection of photographs is a celebration of the wild beauty that still exists in an island chain that staggers under the impact of over six million tourists a year. Each island's section is preceded by a story to introduce and set the stage for the images that follow. It is frequently said that many things of great value are not truly appreciated until they are gone forever. That statement couldn't be more true for our islands that harbor a wealth of endangered species as well as many natural wonders that have as yet escaped the developer's bulldozer. In appreciation of their accomplishments in this regard, a percentage of the proceeds from the sale of this book will be donated to the Nature Conservancy of Hawai'i.

Acknowledgements

A special note of thanks goes out to the following people: Lynne Meyer for typesetting and design, Linda Bottari of Toppan, Ann Fielding and Rusty Lillico for use of their slides, Eric Komori and Muffet Jourdane of the Bishop Museum Anthropology Department, Dr. Loyal Mehrhoff of the Bishop Museum Botany Department, and to my many hiking and adventuring partners, especially Olga Caldwell, Don Fox, Bill Pfeiffer, Sophie Twigg-Smith, David Loo, Priit Vesilind, Kimie Hirabayashi, and Don and Sandy Harvey.

Notes on the Hawaiian Language

The twelve-letter Hawaiian alphabet contains seven consonants and five vowels. Vowel pronunciation for "a,e,i,o" and "u" is "ah, ay, ee, oh" and "oo." Long vowels (with macrons i.e. "ā") are stressed. Consonants are similar to English except for "w" which is more of a "v" sound especially after "i" and "e" as in " 'ewa" and "iwi." An initial "w" or when "w" follows "a," can vary from a "w" to a "v " sound among different speakers. There are no silent letters. The glottal stop or brief pause between vowels is an important feature of the language and sounds like "oh-oh" in words such as Ko'olau for example. A common mistake even among local residents is to incorrectly pronounce vowels so one hears Hanalulu instead of Honolulu. Also the glottal stop in words like Kaua'i and Moloka'i is often omitted.

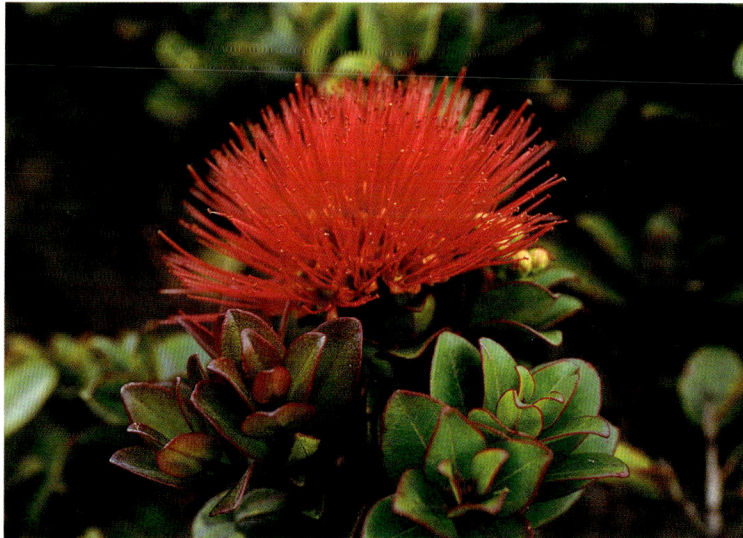

Varying in color from common red to infrequent yellow, the 'ōhi'a lehua flower is the symbol of the Hawaiian forest.

Table of Contents

Powerful forces of stream erosion on the Koʻolau shield volcano created this great windward pali. This view extends along the face with the head of Kalihi Valley in the center. Not included in the photograph is the ugly, concrete scar of the H3 freeway project which lies below.

The Island Of

O'AHU

O'AHU

Hawai'i

Breaking through a cloud layer, the sun lights up the pali across from Kōnāhuanui.

The Island of O'ahu

◢ ◢ ◢ ◢ ◢ ◢ ◢ ◢ ◢ ◢ ◢

Ko'olau Mist

It was probably not the smartest decision of our Ko'olau hiking career. The idea on this cool, cloudy day had been to follow up the stream as far as we could safely go. We had already negotiated past a few small waterfalls without much difficulty. However, with each succeeding obstacle overcome, we could count on a new challenge awaiting us as the typical, plunge-pool Hawaiian stream ascended the narrow valley in step-wise fashion up into the mist.

Now, just above to the right, the stream poured over a mossy, polished lip and plunged approximately 40 feet into a larger pool. One small 'ōhi'a tree projecting out over the drop would hopefully secure our ascent from our somewhat shaky stance to the safety of the steam above.

Don turned to me with a questioning look, "Well, what do you think? Shall we go for it?"

The tree looked like it would hold, but the real question was about the fact that we could well be committing ourselves to a one-way trip because a return via the same route would not be easy. We couldn't really tell what lay ahead except that the next waterfall could end up being impassable, leaving us in a bit of a bind.

Just behind me, Mike asked the unanswerable question:

"Just out of curiosity, how far do you think it is to the top?"

Each one of these streams had its source somewhere near the Ko'olau crest, but there was no way of knowing whether or not we would even-tually be staring at a dead-end, 100-foot waterfall.

Showing the wisdom of an experienced Ko'olau veteran, I chipped in, "Well, I think we're pretty close. It would be a chance for a great loop trip. Once we hit the top, we could go along the crest and come down on one of the next ridge trails without any problems."

So it was that after bypassing one more moderate sized waterfall, fortunately without much difficulty, the ghostly mist-enshrouded Ko'olau crest was in sight. It was real high because we could see that our gamble had paid off as we picked our way along the last small traces of the stream. Also accounting for the magical feeling, was the knowledge that all around us was native, wet-forest vegetation. The cool mist rushed by our faces and occasionally the unmistakable rusty-gate call of the i'iwi could be heard. This native honeycreeper, with its striking curved bill, is sighted less and less frequently these days and usually only in the more remote reaches of the Ko'olaus such as this very spot. We passed small, healthy loulu palms and 'ōhi'a dwarfed by constant exposure to the tradewinds. In the distance, small birds with red plumage flitted here and there through the foliage.

Suddenly, on a downed hāpu'u trunk, I saw the exquisite yellow and green striped shell of a tree snail. These creatures, once so common, are now very seldom seen. It was easy to see why they were once avidly collected, but the real culprit in their near demise was an introduced cannibalistic snail. Crouched down among the tangle of 'ie'ie vine and 'ama'u fern, I tried to get still maintain sharp focus. Close-up photography in frequently overcast Ko'olau summit regions is always a challenge, and I didn't want to blow this opportunity. (You guessed it, I did ! As a result, unfortunately, you will see no picture of *Achatinella* on these pages.)

Up on the main ridge at last, we took a break for lunch in a small, grassy clearing bordered by small moss and fern draped 'ōhi'a and lapalapa with its incongruous, fluttering aspen-like leaves. We were literally sitting in the clouds looking out over the pali where on a clear day the magnificent panorama of windward O'ahu and ocean would ordinarily be spread out before us. Just then, as if on cue, the grey swirling void began to open up, and just for a moment, we had our view. This phenomenon was a relatively frequent reward for patience on these kinds of Ko'olau days, and it was always a special thrill. I was reminded of an earlier overnight trip where we had been sitting in such a place watching the golden, fading, last light of day play across the fluted pali cliffs, while at the same time hearing the clear strains of Hawaiian music from a backyard jam session drift upward from far below.

For the next several hours, we picked our way through the ridge-top vegetation as we followed the ups and downs of the main Ko'olau crest. Our route, which was primarily used by pigs, plus an occasional human, followed the path of least resistance meaning that most of the time we were a foot or two away from the edge of the pali. With the view down the 2,000 foot face obscured by clouds and with the softening effect of 'uki sedge grass, 'ama'u fern, 'ōhelo and small kanawao on the cliff edge, it all seemed deceptively safe, but actually, it was no place to be careless. There was often a kind of false sense of security that would not have been the case if we were walking along a similar sheer but rocky face.

At times we encountered an outbreak of *Clidemia*, the obnoxious plant that was introduced to Hawai'i by a botanist, of all people. Brought in as an ornamental plant, it quickly spread, choking out native species in the process. On some O'ahu trails it was not unusual to see head-high thickets of *Clidemia*, and the Sierra Club had worked especially hard to get rid of this pest, or at least limit it to O'ahu. Nevertheless, like other exotic species, it has run rampant, and its eradication appears to be a losing and frustrating battle. Significant amounts of money have been appropriated by the legislature to search for an insect antidote, but unfortunately, the state leaders have been slow to release the funds.

Just after going over the top of a small peak on the ridge, I happened to glance to the leeward side and noticed that the clouds seemed to be opening up a little. Looking past the outline of ghostly, twisted 'ōhi'a on the steep ridge profiled in front of me, I watched the clouds swirl and shift until suddenly, a gap appeared in the center.

"Hey, you guys, take a look at this," I exclaimed as Don and Mike pulled up beside me.

Framed in the grey mist was a view of the high-rise towers of Waikiki with the afternoon sun glinting off the sea beyond.

"Spooky, isn't it?" said Mike.

"You know, it's like we slipped back in time," remarked Don.

We all had the same thoughts as we stared out at the apparition that had opened up before us. Here in this primitive and almost pristine location, it was as if we were *po'e kahiko*, people of old, seeing a vision of what was to come. It was a fitting subject for a painting which might be able to capture this spectral scene. However, after a couple of quick photographic attempts, the grey curtain dropped on that memorable image.

At that point we were quite close to our connecting exit ridge. The final section along the crest involved a short, steep descent. Here the leeward headwall had eroded quite close to the main ridge, resulting in a narrow spine with an attention-getting drop on the right to go with the formidable green wall of the pali itself falling away into the clouds on the left. Negotiating this part of the route called for a low center of gravity and a straddle appeared to be the best approach, especially with gusts of wind threatening to launch us into space. So down we came, slowing ourselves with handfuls of 'uki: a technique that was practical if not classic.

Mike, who was a seasoned veteran of mainland trails and peaks, and on his first Ko'olau trek, was the last to come down. As he reached the more level, broader section of the ridge where we stood, he looked at us with a smile and said,

"You know, you guys really are crazy."

As we headed back down to civilization, I thought to myself that I was glad we were a little bit crazy on this occasion, especially since all the main obstacles were safely behind us. It had been an unforgettable Ko'olau day.

The Ko'olau mists open up briefly to reveal the high-rise towers of sunlit Waikiki.

Above: Near the lower of the twin summits of Kōnāhuanui, the clouds swirl over the crest. This peak, highest of the Ko'olau range, is often enveloped in clouds on many normal tradewind days.

The clouds disperse, and the tantalizing glimpses of windward O'ahu become a full-fledged reality.

Cloud shadows stand out in the brilliant mirror of morning sun reflected off the Kaiwi (Moloka'i) channel.

Left: An eroded rib on the flank of Koko Crater provides an unusual route to the summit which lies on the southwestern rim. This crater is probably the most recent of a series of secondary eruptions that also produced Diamond Head and other familiar Honolulu landmarks.

Sunset's golden light bathes the waters of Maunalua Bay where whaling vessels once anchored while taking on provisions from the inland valleys.

High above a restless sea, hikers pick their way up the rough slopes of Makapu'u Head.

Left: Along the base of the Makapu'u Head sea cliff, quiet pools and strange lava formations are to be found on the shelf above thundering waves.

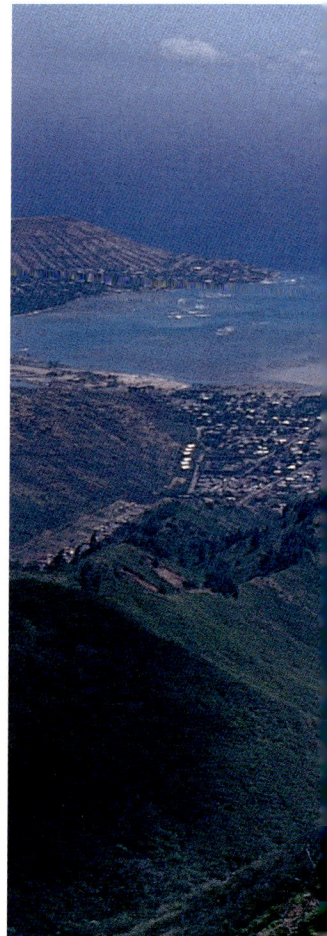

Right: Two hikers near their goal as they approach the top of one of the ridges above Niu Valley.

The view from one of the narrow gaps in this dry section of the Koʻolau Crest extends down Hahaʻione Valley toward Maunalua Bay and Koko Head.

Heading downward (center) toward Waialae Nui with views of multi-hued greens carpeting the ridges and valleys below, memories of spectacular windward sights remain (top left & right, bottom left). Lingering at the top on such beautiful, clear days gives one the bonus of a sunset seen from the heights (bottom right).

Hāpu'u, 'ōhi'a and other sturdy, wind-resistant, native vegetation cling to the narrow crest while fluted, sheer walls drop down to Waimanalo.

Here the Koʻolau pali sweeps around the scoured head of a former separate valley and extends toward the southeastern tip of Oʻahu.

Sunset's finale illuminates the pali with a soft, golden glow.

Striking Ka'au crater is another example of one of the later secondary eruptions in the Honolulu area. Near the head of Palolo Valley, it is especially well-seen from the Lanipō trail (above) or from the Ko'olau crest (below).

Some examples of the endemic rain forest flora to be found in the Koʻolaus:

Lapalapa
Cheirodendron platyphyllum

Kāmakahala
Labordia spp.

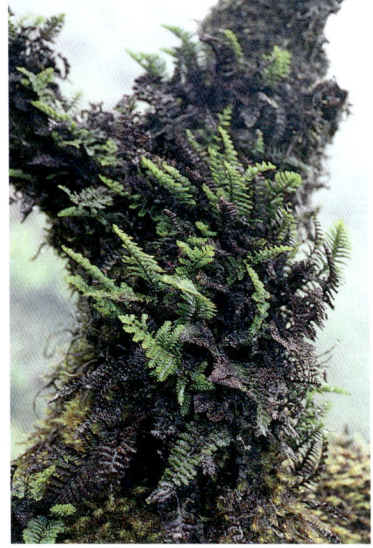

Fern and moss encased ʻōhiʻa

Lobelias
Trematolobelia singularis

Lobelias (Koliʻi)
Trematolobelia macrostachys

Lobelias
Rollandia augustifolia

Loulu
Pritchardia spp.

Kōlea
Myrsine sandwicensis

Kanawao
Broussaisia arguta

23

Upper Koʻolau ridges frame the Tantalus area with Manoa Valley on the left and Nuʻuanu Valley on the right.

This high Kōnāhuanui ridge vantage point looks down Nuʻuanu Valley with Pearl Harbor in the background.

Shadows cover upper Nuʻuanu while the lower section and its surrounding ridges lie in sunshine. The water now seen in Nuʻuanu stream and reservoir was once responsible for carving out this wide valley.

Vegetation seems to cover any sign of a trail where this smiling hiker pauses briefly before climbing up into the mists of Kōnāhuanui.

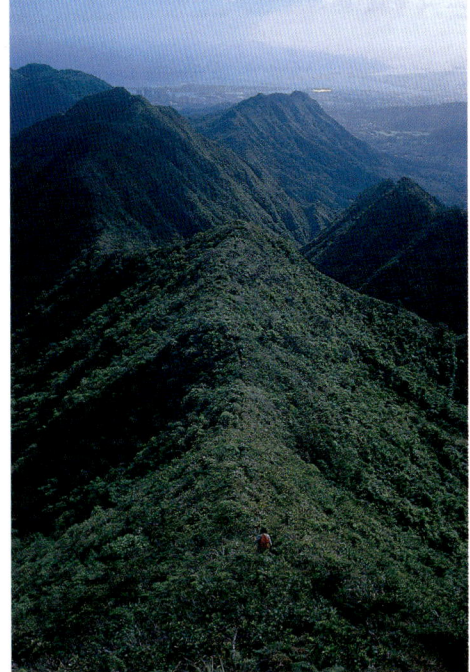

A succession of wonderful views accompanies the hiker's descent along the ridge from Kōnāhuanui.

Another spectacular Hawaiian sunset is enjoyed here from a vantage point above upper Nuʻuanu.

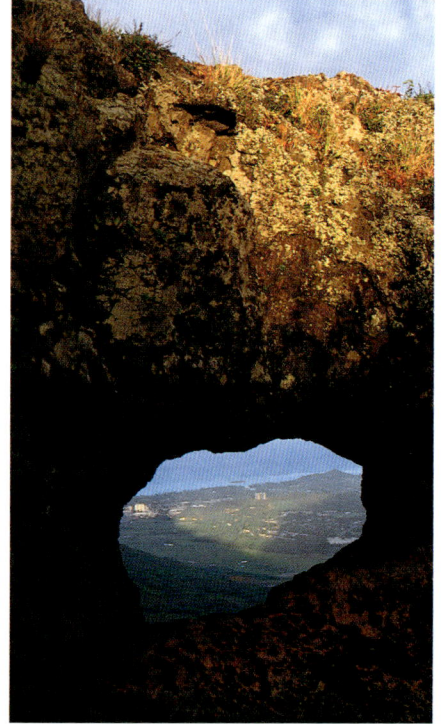

Top right: Whether due to endless battering on soft rock by wind and rain or the result of a legendary warrior's spear, the Nu'uanu Pali puka (hole) can be seen at a certain point when driving up the Pali highway toward Kailua. Top left: It is also visible from a greater distance (see box) as in this photograph from across the valley. Even more dramatic is the view of windward O'ahu obtained by looking directly through while feeling the blast of the tradewinds (below right). The last rays of sun slant across the sheer precipice above the Nu'uanu Pali highway (below left).

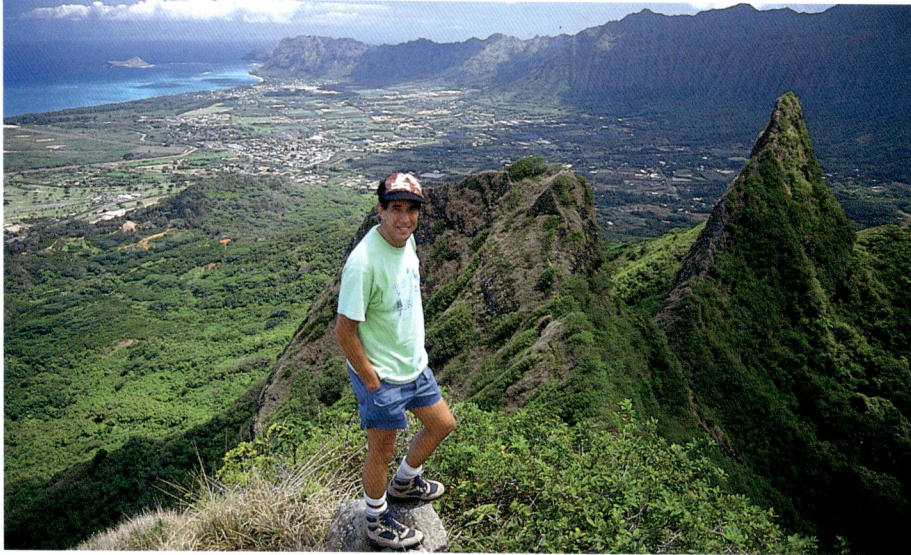

Olomana—a peak experience near Kailua: The rewards of this relatively short hike include some breathtaking views toward the ocean in addition to a panoramic perspective on the great fluted wall of the Koʻolau pali. In legend, Olomana was named for a giant that jumped from Kauaʻi to this peak.

As seen from Olomana, the Mokulua Islands sit side by side in a sea of brilliant blue.

From the smaller of the two islands, a much different view in the opposite direction finds Olomana Peak blending into the background in the center.

A sparkling early morning finds a deserted Mokulua beach (left). Views from the summits give an unusual perspective towards Kailua Bay (top left) and in the direction of Waimanalo (top right). The channel between the two islands can provide some ridable waves, especially for kayakers (bottom right). The water on the backside of both Mokuluas is usually rough and turbulent due to swells and backwash. On a calm day, there are coves and channels to explore and interesting rock formations to be seen. Bottom left: Paddling home after some more Mokulua adventures.

Old-time Hawaiians would probably cringe a little at the common name of Bird Shit Island for Mōkōlea Rock (left). Although appropriately nick-named due to the accumulation of guano on the leeward side, the real name is actually a short-ened form of Moku (island) and Kōlea (the Pacific Golden Plover). At one time, kōleas from large colonies in the Kailua area used to fly out to these rocks at night. This remarkable migratory bird (top right) makes an annual journey of over 2,400 miles to breeding grounds in Alaska. Now these rocks are home to brown and black noddies (right and below right). Turbulent seas on the outside are the rule (below left), but the paddle back offers a remarkable panoramic view of the Koʻolau range.

Above: On the way to visit Mokumanu, the kayaker passes through chaotic seas with large swells rebounding off the cliffs of Ulupa'u Head. Below: Mokumanu, an eroded tuff cone, is a State Seabird Sanctuary with thousands of terns, shearwaters, boobies and other seabirds periodically in residence (below).

Waves glisten outside of Mokumanu in this view looking back toward Ulupa'u Head and the Mōkapu peninsula.

This yawning sea cave on the north side of Mokumanu can be explored on calmer days.

Dwarfed by the massive bulk of Ulupa'u Head, an intrepid kayaker paddles back to Kailua Bay against the prevailing winds.

A twisted 'ōhi'a hangs out over the edge of the Lanihuli ridge. The head of Kalihi Valley lies below with windward O'ahu beginning to be visible over the Wilson tunnel pali.

A dense, healthy growth of hapu'u ferns and other endemic, wet-forest plants cling to a high, steep slope. Lanihuli is the peak visible in the background.

Left: High above Kalihi Valley which lies to the left, a hiker on the upper Bowman trail picks his way through the ridgetop 'ōhi'a.

A cloud layer hangs above the Ko'olaus from a lofty viewpoint above and to the left of Moanalua Valley.

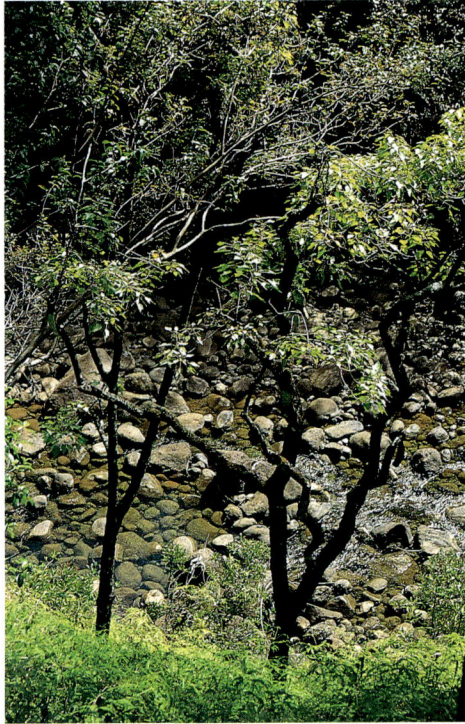

Rosettes of leaves form an eye-catching silhouette.

Sunlight plays among the stones and pools of an Oʻahu stream with its overhanging canopy of kukui trees.

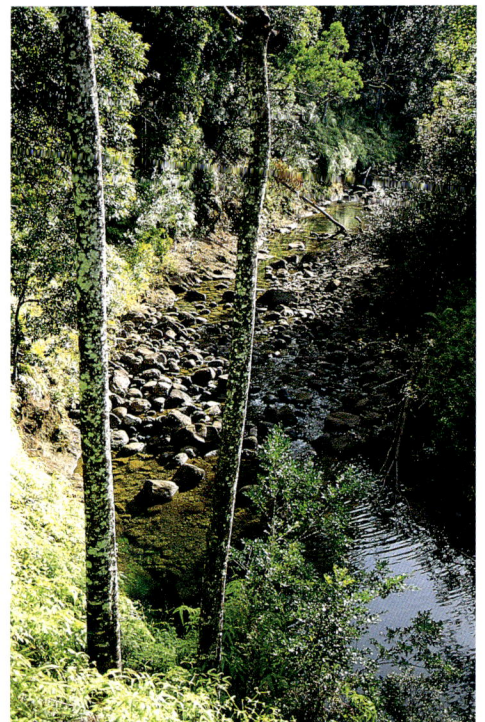

A quiet, inviting pool tempts any fortunate visitor to this idyllic spot. These streams can be peaceful and slow-moving, but with sudden tropical downpours, they can become raging torrents, presenting potential dangers to hikers in narrow valleys.

Morning light reflects off the water of this stream winding down through a seldom-visited central Oʻahu valley.

Poised high above the Pacific on Pu'u Piei near Kahana Bay, this hiker seems to be a step away from disaster.

Beautiful views of Kualoa Regional Park and its fish ponds reward the climber to such a promontory near the top of Mokoli'i Island (Chinaman's Hat). In legend, Mokoli'i is the tail of a mo'o (lizard or dragon) killed by the goddess Hi'iaka.

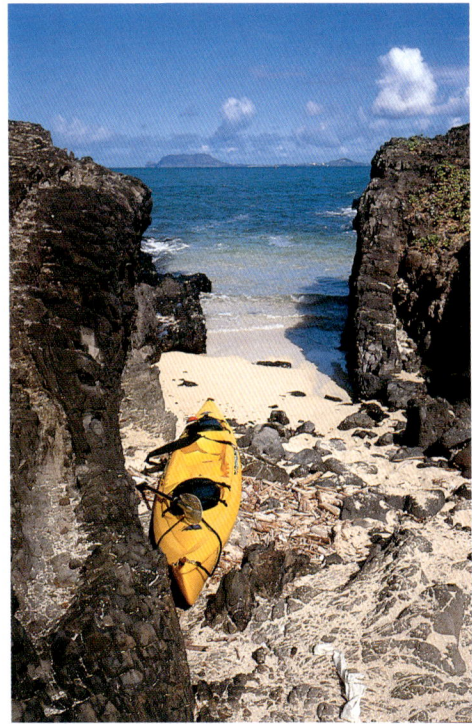

Kapapa Island on the outer side of a large reef in Kaneohe Bay makes an interesting and scenic destination for kayakers.

On the back side of Mokoli'i is a custom designed kayak harbor and landing.

Viewpoints provide panoramic vistas across the Schofield plain to Haleiwa (above left) and toward the center of O'ahu, the Pearl Harbor area and the distant Ko'olau range (above right).

Bare rocky outcrops such as this one just to the north of Pu'u Kanehoa are spectacular vantage points.

At times when the tradewinds weaken, usually clear peaks can be enveloped in swirling clouds.

Left: The great eroded western slope of the Waianae Range, older and drier now than the Ko'olaus, is nearly as impressive.

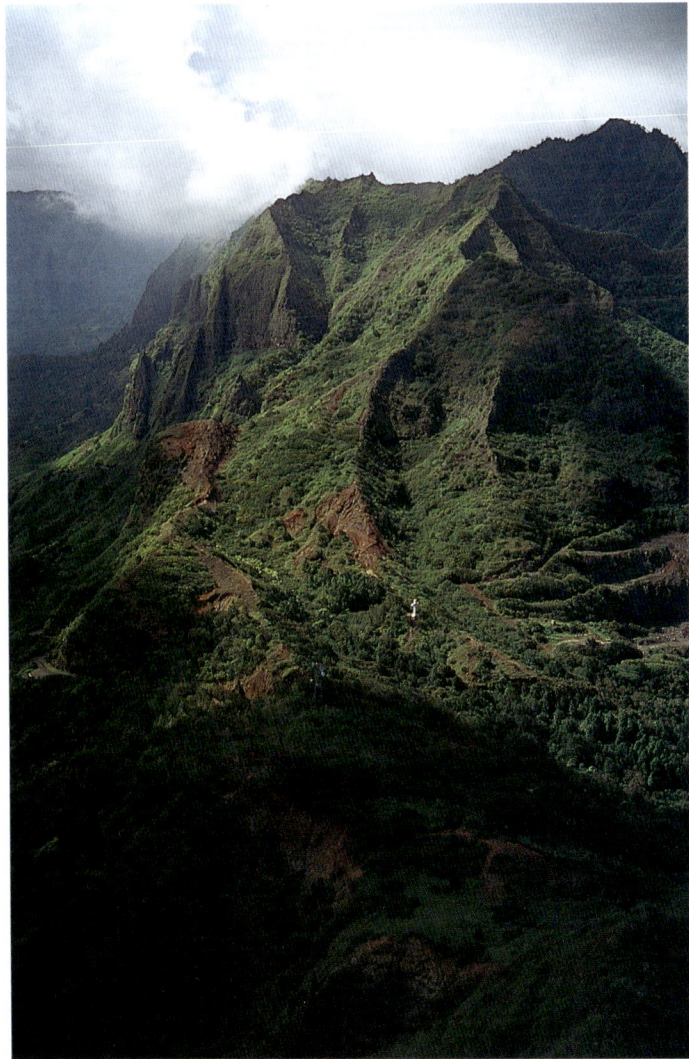

Right: Sun shines on the huge cross on Kolekole Pass with the slopes beyond rising upward to Pu'u Kalena, the second highest peak on O'ahu. Further to the north is its loftiest, Ka'ala (4,025 ft.), where the broad summit plateau and bog represent a minimally altered remnant of the original Waianae volcano.

On a clear day, the prize at the end of a 4-hour hike on the Manana trail is a magnificent view of central windward O'ahu, especially the reefs and landmarks of the Kaneohe Bay area (top left and left). Further to the south along the ridge, more of Waihee Valley comes into view as in this picture where loulu palms dot the foreground slopes above the drop-off (above right).

Sunlit ridge above Waihee Valley.

Kipapa trail summit.

Looking into the great chasm of Waihee Valley.

Sampling the Central Koʻolaus

ʻŌhiʻa and the leeward view.

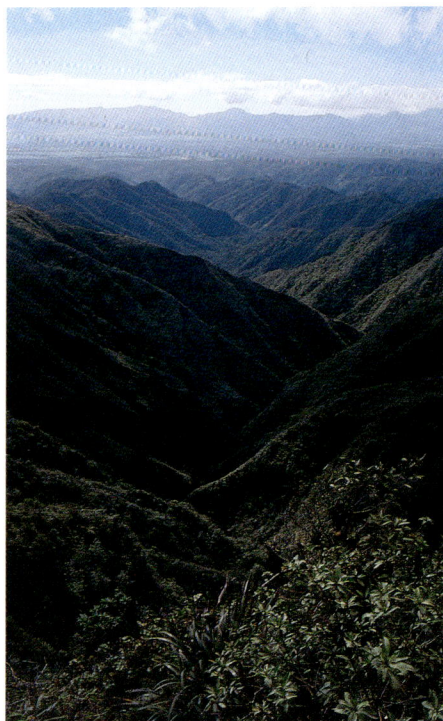

To the west above the head of a Koʻolau Valley.

42

A spectacular vantage point gives this hiker an inspiring view on a perfect day near the Poamoho trail summit.

Two pools sparkle in the sun below the Poamoho cabin.

Looking downward toward beautiful Kahana Valley, it is nice to know that it is preserved as a state park.

Painting, photography and relaxing in the sun are all possible ways to celebrate a wonderfully clear day at Poamoho (top left & center). Framed by some hardy loulu palms, this photograph looks back toward the Poamoho summit from the north (top right). A stone marker was recently built just on the leeward side of the crest giving trail mileage (bottom left) and a pertinent message (bottom right).

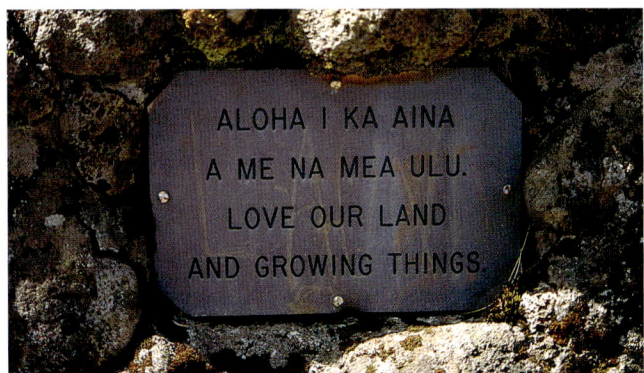

ALOHA I KA AINA
A ME NA MEA ULU.
LOVE OUR LAND
AND GROWING THINGS.

45

Kayak Adventures

Trail's end at Awa'awapuhi provides this unequalled aerial view of a unique valley.

The Island Of

KAUA'I

KAUA'I

Hawai'i

Exhilaration above two valleys: A hiker celebrates a spectacular vantage point.

The Island of Kaua'i

▲ ▲ ▲ ▲ ▲ ▲ ▲ ▲ ▲ ▲ ▲ ▲

Awa'awapuhi Rainbow

The great eel was thrown high in the air as the ocean convulsed in a mighty explosion of steam and trapped gases. It came down on a cooling river of lava on a slope above the boiling sea. Thrashing and twisting its massive body, the pūhi struggled to escape. However, it succeeded only in sinking itself deeper into the black, malevolent mass, and then, after one final hopeless effort, it lay still. In the years to follow, the sea rose and receded, and the rains came, sculpturing the new shore and eroding the cliffs and intervening valleys. And one such valley, formed originally by the great eel's body, became known as Awa'awapuhi.

Although in translation the name means "ginger valley," variations on this story of the eel have been told by Hawaiians to explain the shape of Awa'awapuhi which is one of the most spectacular of Kaua'i's Nā Pali Coast valleys. I was always fascinated by it, partly because of its eye-catching name, and also on account of its inaccessibility.

Seen from the ocean, Awa'awapuhi stream drops over a formidable, low cliff onto a small, uninviting boulder beach, while above, multi-colored orange and black eroded basaltic crags guard the valley's entrance. Imposing walls sweep upward on either side culminating in massive, fluted green cliffs that soar over 3,000 feet at the rear of the valley.

On a steep bluff to the right of the stream, the rock wall of a substantial platform can be seen when looking up from the sea. The most likely route into the valley may well have been via a trail which originated in the adjacent valley of Nu'alolo 'Āina and wound below the cliffs passing this distinctive structure. In contrast to narrow Awa'awapuhi, extensive terracing and stone platforms have been found in Nu'alolo 'Āina, indicating significant Hawaiian usage at one time. Besides using the rough boulder beach in the calmer summer months, access into Nu'alolo 'Āina itself at one time involved a spectacular ladder-assisted climb up a vertical cliff from the shallow valley of Nu'alolo Kai to the west.

Nowadays, most views between the precipitous walls of Awa'awapuhi come from tourist helicopter flights. However, there is another way which results in a trip to one of the most dramatic and breathtaking viewpoints in Hawai'i. Descending 3-1/4 miles from the Kōke'e road above, the Awa'awapuhi trail is an unforgettable experience, especially for first-time hikers.

The first part of the trail is a pleasant, gradual descent through mixed koa and 'ōhi'a forest where, unfortunately, another pest like *clidemia* is found draped over branches and small trees. Banana poka is an introduced vine which has flourished in some areas of Kaua'i, and to the uninitiated, it looks attractive because of its pink flower. But once again as in the case of *clidemia* its effect on native vegetation has been devastating.

Hoping not to lose too much altitude as you descend, occasional glimpses of blue ocean appear as the forest begins to thin out a little. However, there is no hint of the visual spectacle that is in store at this point. The trail follows a dry ridge for a while, and then switches back down a shady section on the side of a small valley. Nearby, a trail branches off which eventually links up with a parallel trail dropping down to the head of Nu'alolo 'Āina. Continuing straight ahead, you become aware that you are getting close to the edge of a pali; ahead there is a more open grassy area with only an occasional tree and more expansive ocean views.

Suddenly, you find yourself standing at the top of an eroded narrow ridge with a few rocky outcrops, and an unbelievable panorama is spread out before you. To the right is the incredible chasm of Awa'awapuhi and on the left is the broader upper valley of Nu'alolo 'Āina. A cautious descent a short distance down this ridge, which eventually divides the two valleys, brings you to a point where you can literally sit and look down between your feet at the sun glinting on pools in Awa'awapuhi stream 3,000 feet below. White-tailed tropic birds, koa'e kea, soar and play in the updrafts sweeping up the pali. The sea far below looks deceptively glassy and calm. Goats can be seen at times on the ridge further down. Although it is interesting to watch their exploits on these cliffs, they have not been kind to native vegetation and have contributed significantly to erosion problems.

The awesome beauty of this view is disturbed with regularity by Kaua'i's ever-present commercial helicopter flights. As one who has had a fascination with helicopters dating back to Vietnam days, in this setting I can only find them an annoying aggravation. They have been restricted somewhat and most of the time no longer buzz the treetops, irritating hikers and terrorizing the native forest bird population. However, occasionally some pilots still seem to take liberties with their airspace privileges.

The impact of choppers was brought clearly into focus at the time of our first visit to this magnificent vantage point. We were eating lunch when gradually we noticed that something was different. Suddenly it all made sense. It was the stillness! The helicopter pilots took lunch breaks, too! We had an hour or so to enjoy this inspirational sight in peace and quiet. What a bonus! But yet, on this particular day, there was more. We had some brief showers, ua li'i li'i, on the way down, and once again a short and refreshing light tradewind shower passed over us. Quickly the sun broke through, and we were treated to the most spectacular rainbow I've ever seen! Arching up from Nu'alolo and disappearing into the shady depths of Awa'awapuhi, it seemed almost to complete a full circle.

Try as I might, I knew I was photographically overmatched in trying to capture the image of this stunning rainbow. Even in our islands where rainbows are commonplace, this one was unequalled. We sat there in awe at the beauty of the scene. Then, as it faded, in the distance there was the unwelcome sound of approaching helicopters. By the time they arrived, the rainbow was gone, and the spell was broken. Later, leaving Awa'awapuhi behind as we headed reluctantly back up to the world of tour vans and buses, we realized that we had been fortunate spectators at one of nature's finest moments.

Feral goats as well as humans seem to enjoy these remarkable sights. Unfortunately they don't provide their own food, and the loss of native vegetation and associated erosion detract from the enjoyment of watching their agile performances on the heights. Fencing and hunting offer some hope for control of these animals first brought to Hawaii by Captain Cook in 1778.

Sunshine and a passing tradewind shower create a memorable rainbow arching up over Nu'alolo 'Āina.

Clouds sweep up over the pali as hikers gaze downward at the stunning precipice on either side.

Pointing the bow downwind, a kayaker starts an unforgettable trip down the Nā Pali coast.

Shafts of late afternoon light slant across the Kalalau pali as the weary hiker nears the valley. Traversing eleven miles of magnificent sea cliffs and coastal valleys, this route remains one of the classic wilderness experiences in the Hawaiian islands.

The journey nearly over, the wonderful sight of Kalalau Beach welcomes the hiker. Ever popular, especially during the summer months, camping at Kalalau is by permit only and stays are limited.

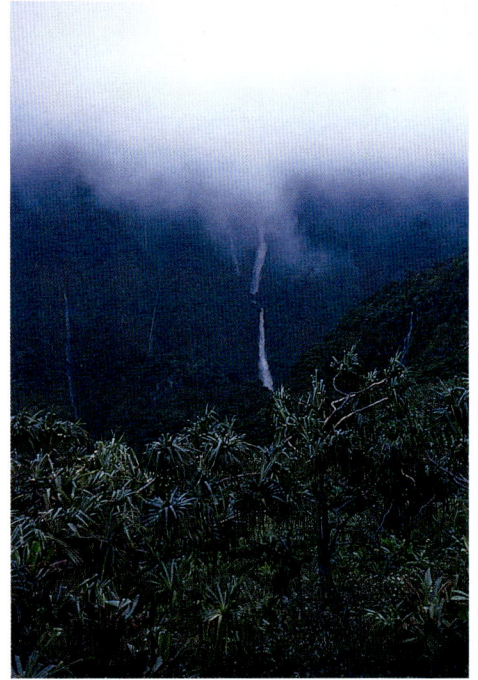

Winds buffet hiker and hala tree on a winter day above Hanakāpīʻai Beach. Water conditions here can be extremely dangerous with hazardous surf and notorious currents.

Heavy rains can bring hundreds of waterfalls to life on short notice as huge volumes of water pour down the pali, recreating the forces of its origin.

In contrast to the stormy scene above, the sun shines on a picturesque beach on the coast.

Taking advantage of the prevailing wind and swells, it's full speed ahead to Kalalau.

Transit through this remarkable cave with its own inner waterfall can be made in either direction when seas are relatively calm.
(Photo by Rusty Lillico)

Kalalau Beach — the centerpiece of Nā Pali Coastal State Park: In the mid-sixties, it was still possible to camp here and see only your own footprints on this beautiful long beach. Nowadays, the visitor will have some company, but the incredible scenery and sense of remoteness are still there.

Shadows fall across the cliffs above Kalalau Beach. The last Hawaiian inhabitants around the turn of the century made tapa from the wauke or paper mulberry trees growing on the plateau visible here to the left of Hoʻoleʻa Falls.

As the sun falls toward the horizon, a diffuse warm golden glow lights up the sharp ridges and spines of the upper Kalalau ramparts.

Dropping over the cliffs near the western end of the beach, Ho'ole'a Falls is a scenic delight and a source of drinking water.

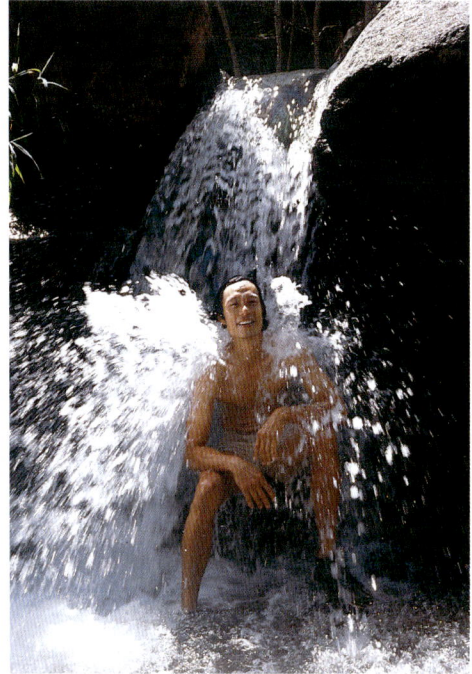

An invigorating fresh water shower and massage is always a welcome highlight on a hike up one of Nā Pali's valleys.

The pali to the east is silhouetted against the sky as evening comes to Kalalau.

Mornings arrive at Kalalau Beach with the anticipation of another day's adventure. When the ocean is calm, it can be a good time to enjoy a swim before tradewinds and currents become stronger.

Caves at the western end provide shelter and were once a semi-permanent residence for free spirits who frequented the valley prior to the state's management policy in 1980. Some caves like this one around the corner from the main beach are really wet caves which will have a temporary summer-time addition of sand.

Sunsets are a time to reflect on the timeless beauty of this wilderness setting (above). It is also prime time for photographers who must try not to use up too much of their film on these visual spectaculars! (left)

After launching from Kalalau, the kayaker can take a break and admire the view as the beach begins to disappear behind the cliffs.

Aided by wind and a following sea, the run past Honopū begins.

A landing is possible here, and the visitor can hike over to the western part of the beach beneath this massive arch in the lava barrier between the twin beaches.

Off shore again, the very photogenic hanging valley of Honopū becomes visible. As one might expect, even in this remote location with difficult access, archeological studies indicate that Hawaiians used the valley. There is no evidence of any other earlier residents despite the catchy popular name of the Valley of the Lost Tribe.

The unique "topless" cave with its eroded, open-air roof and a small island in the center is a fascinating highlight on the coast past Honopū.

Looking carefully up above the multihued cliffs of Awaʻawapuhi, the rocky spine below the end of the upper trail (see page 50) can be seen. The valley's stream falls over a forbidding cliff to a small, rough boulder beach apparently barring direct access.

From a ledge below the cliffs guarding the old land route to Nuʻalolo ʻĀina, the view back along the coast extends all the way to Keʻe Beach where the journey begins. Note the brisk tradewinds blowing down the coast to the west in this picture taken in the early afternoon.

Often, mists can rapidly shroud the upper pali in ghostly outlines and then can just as quickly disperse to reveal stunning views.

An 'ōhi'a tree captures moisture from mists sweeping up from the void below (upper right).

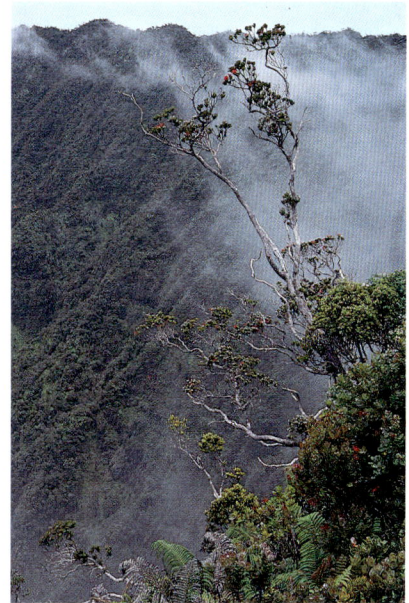

A trail heading down into the Alaka'i swamp promises verdant native vegetation as well as muddy feet (lower right).

In the Kōke'e area, a variety of routes are available encouraging visits to quiet, clear streams like this one (below).

Not content to simply tumble down the pali in a single cascade, amazing Wailele Falls catches the tradewinds and fans out along the cliff. This view shows only the lower third of the whole waterfall which comes from high above off the eastern end of the Oloku'i sea cliff.

The Island Of

MOLOKA‘I

MOLOKA‘I

Hawai‘i

The highest sea cliffs in the world fall over 3,400 feet to the ocean along this stretch of Moloka'i's magnificent north coast. Evidence suggests that wave and stream erosion were their major creators. Because of their sheer height, it was first thought that these towering cliffs must have been formed at least partially by faulting.

The Island of Moloka'i

▲ ▲ ▲ ▲ ▲ ▲ ▲ ▲ ▲ ▲ ▲ ▲

Anapūhi Cave

Sea caves seem to be designed with the kayaker in mind. These creations, constantly battered by big winter waves, are generally located at the base of relatively inaccessible sea cliffs. As northwestern Pacific winter storms subside and the ocean becomes more reasonable, exploration of the great variety of Hawaiian sea caves becomes possible. Some of the larger caves such as those on the Nā Pali coast of Kaua'i are sizable enough for a visit by bigger watercraft like inflatable Zodiaks. However, smaller ocean kayaks, either inflatable or hard-shell, provide the optimal way to safely experience the unique beauty of these mysterious places.

Venturing into the yawning, dark opening of a sea cave while trying to judge the mood of the ocean that created it never fails to be a special thrill for the adventurous. Once inside, listening to the squawk of disturbed sea birds and feeling the rise and fall of the entering swell, you have the sensation of being a privileged guest of the ocean gods who have called a brief time-out to allow you to see up close the work of some very powerful forces. Many sea caves were created by repeated pounding of a section of softer rock at the waterline, while some were originally lava tubes which have been enlarged. Because rainfall is a constant on these coasts, waterfalls are frequently present in the vicinity. Two caves on Kaua'i feature waterfalls, one providing an invigorating fresh water shower as you enter and the other having eroded through a side wall with an associated shaft of brilliant sunlight. Also on Kaua'i is the much photographed "topless" cave where part of the roof has collapsed and the visitor bursts through the entrance into the daylight of a large, open chamber. Many caves dead-end in darkness, and some have secondary chambers where thrill seekers can try and time the waves to negotiate past a menacing low-roofed section. Best of all are a few caves where there is an exit as well as an entrance. The most remarkable of this type is Anapūhi Cave on Moloka'i's spectacular north coast.

From Halawa Valley on the eastern end to the peninsula of Kalaupapa, the wild north shore of Moloka'i is the grand crescendo of the action of waves and water in Hawai'i. Here are located the highest sea cliffs in the world and the two magnificent valleys of Wailau and Pelekunu. The Oloku'i plateau between these valleys is one of few remaining pristine sites as it has remained inaccessible to the ravages of feral pigs and goats due to soaring, precipitous cliffs on all sides. Incredible waterfalls plummet thousands of feet into the sea, and their number will dramatically increase after a storm. This coast was first brought to people's attention by Audrey Sutherland's intrepid solo kayak trips in the sixties (1). Fortunately, it remains relatively undisturbed because access is so difficult except for a brief period of time during the summer months. Furthermore, the Nature Conservancy is now Pelekunu's guardian, as this organization has increased its holdings on Moloka'i to include this beautiful valley.

A kayaker ventures into the eel's lair.

First views of this incredible coastline have considerable impact. I vividly recall an April voyage on the old Seaflite hydrofoil after several days of very rainy weather. We cruised along the coast, and all the passengers, faces pressed to the windows on that side of the boat, were treated to the awesome view of what seemed like thousands of waterfalls pouring down the cliffs. It was a breathtaking and yet primeval sight made more so by the overhanging grey clouds obscuring the cliff tops. It was as though a curtain had been raised revealing the very forces of creation at work. Hawaiian music was usually played over the stereo system on these trips, but someone had put on some inspirational Wagnerian classical piece. It seemed particularly appropriate because we were truly seeing a climactic symphony of nature's finest handiwork.

Anapūhi is a remarkable sea cave located in a projecting cliff to the west of Pelekunu valley. A nineteenth century account gives an excellent description:

.....a large entrance cave, its opening extending up to a considerable height of the cliff. As we neared it I was afraid the canoe mast would hinder our entrance, but we did without striking. On entering we first noticed its length within, some thirty fathoms. At first we did not see its opening or exit, but continuing on, there it was, a wide aperture on the left side. We went right inside. It had a distinctive beauty. Its water was deep and its roof very high, being ten fathoms in some places, and less in others. Water trickled

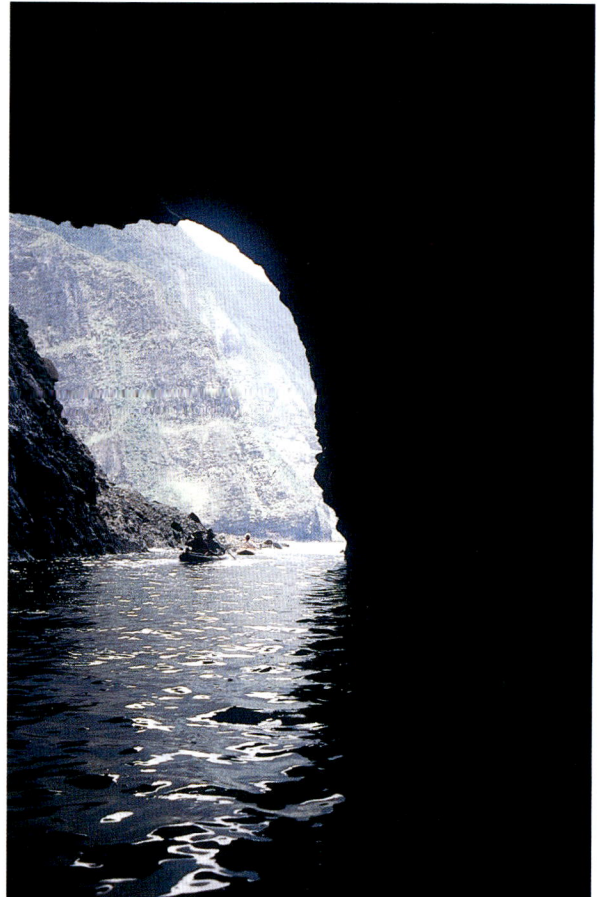

Exiting Anapūhi cave: Nearby is a small, delightful waterfall where the kayaker, with a little maneuvering, can enjoy a refreshing shower and a drink without getting out of the boat.

down from above like rain. It is wide within; four canoes would have no difficulty in maneuvering inside. It is forty fathoms perhaps lengthwise from one opening to the other. The sea-waves had colored it clear to the ceiling, striped and spotted red in some places, while in others, dark gray, green gray, yellow, and shiny black in others. All above was beautiful. The cave was crowded with noios (or sea swallow, Anous stolidus), wild birds, very angry, not at all agreeable to our entering their home. (Hitchcock, 1836) (2).

The cave is not only large, but because of its configuration, morning light slants through the entrance and reflects off the walls, giving the water an electric-blue color. It is Hawaii's version of Capri's famous blue grotto. In addition it comes complete with a fascinating legend to account for some of its features:

It was not uncommon among the very early Hawaiians for a shark to be born of perfectly normal human parents. Such a shark was born to a couple living at Waialua (Moloka'i). This shark was wrapped in ti leaves and taken to the ocean where it was tenderly cared for. As a result of such tender care the shark child grew rapidly. Meanwhile, two normal children were born to this couple, but they continued their care of the eldest, going down to the ocean daily before dawn to feed it.

One day the couple expected to be away from home for the whole day, so they gave the two children the responsibility of feeding their brother. Very early the next day the couple set off, satisfied that all would be well at home. The children, however, being left for the first time without supervision, were soon so engrossed in play that they forgot their older brother. Just about sunset they suddenly remembered, and left their play to hasten to the ocean with his food. The shark, having waited since early morning, was so famished at the delay that he devoured the two children.

When the parents learned the fate of their two children, they immediately sent word to all the island that the shark was not to be fed, but was to starve to death in his punishment for his horrible crime. He had devoured his own flesh and blood! A tabu was then put on all sharks in these Hawaiian waters. All sharks were forbidden to eat of human flesh.

Meanwhile the outcast shark travelled from island to island, seeking food, in vain. He finally returned to Moloka'i, taking refuge in a huge cave in Pelekunu. This cave belonged to an enormous eel (or pūhi) which had been out seeking food. When the eel returned and found his cave occupied, he attacked the intruder and a furious battle followed. So huge were the two fighters, they thrashed their way through the solid rock of the cave, breaking clear through to the other side, thus forming another opening to the cave.

Although the shark fought a gallant battle, the eel was the victor. He bound the body of his foe with strong cord and hauled it up along the side of the cliff, where it was left to rot in the hot sun. A streak of dark red dirt remains at his spot today, where the blood of the shark was supposed to have spilled over the cliff.

In Pelekunu today stands the cave of "Anapūhi" large enough to admit a fairly large boat, which can enter the mouth of the cave and pass clear through and out the other end. And as a result of that old tabu put on all sharks, the old time Hawaiians firmly believe that sharks in these Hawaiian waters will never attack a human, and consequently they have no fear of sharks. (Goodhue, 1952) (3).

Venturing into Anapūhi knowing this story makes your adventure here even more memorable. At the time of our first trip, we decided to take a quick underwater look. Slipping into the almost-glowing, blue water was an eerie feeling, and hearts were pounding as we descended into the eel's lair. But actually, the rocks were scoured pretty clean by the surging waves, and there were only a few fish to be seen. It was kind of a letdown at that point, but we easily decided we weren't too interested in returning for a night dive in this storied place. As in other locations where Hawaiian mythology and reality come close together, we left this unique cave with a mixture of awe and respect. Hopefully, Anapūhi the eel, who was said to be the guardian of the coast from there all the way to Halawa, will be able to help preserve the singular beauty of this magnificent coastline.

(1) Sutherland, Audrey: Paddling My Own Canoe. University of Hawaii Press, 1978
(2) Summers, Catherine C.: Molokai: A Site Survey. Bishop Museum 1974, page 184
(3) Ibid. pages 184-185

Pāpalaua Valley is deep and narrow with impressive waterfalls at the back. Hiking up the stream to the base of the falls is a scramble but well worth it in good weather.

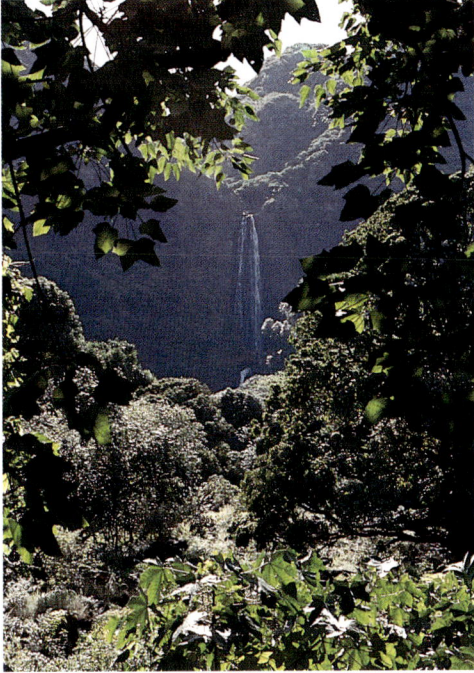

Framed by kukui, Halawa Valley's
Moa'ula Falls beckons the hiker ahead
on a trip to enjoy a swim in the deep pool
at its base.

This view of Pāpalaua Falls in July hints at the energy
that has been at work during winter's rainier months to
create this steep-walled valley.

Waterfalls descend from the plateau
west of Halawa Valley in the typical step-
like Hawaiian plunge pool pattern.

The bay east of Pāpalaua Valley features the striking Keanapuka arch. Resulting from relentless pounding on softer rock, such an arch represents an early stage in the formation of a sea stack. With continued erosion, the roof of the arch eventually collapses leaving a small rocky islet as seen just offshore of many Hawaiian coasts.

Unused to having company in these remote areas, goats are startled by the presence of visitors to the Hāka'a'ano peninsula.

Looking westward along the coast from Hāka'a'ano, the Kalaupapa peninsula is visible in the distance. Created at the base of the sea cliff by a secondary eruption, Kalaupapa was formed much later after activity in Moloka'i's main shield volcano had ceased.

As Polynesian voyagers might have seen it at the time of discovery, the details of Wailau Valley begin to appear in the early morning from the deck of the double-hulled voyaging canoe Hōkūleʻa (top). Wailau, the larger of the two great northern coast valleys, is accessible by sea only in the relative calm of the summer months or by the long, rigorous Wailau trail from the south shore. Below: Here the broad entrance to the valley comes into view as the kayaker approaches from the east.

Summer visitors to Wailau usually land at the eastern end of this wide, picturesque black-sand beach, and local families often camp on the shore near Wailau Stream. Creator of this beautiful valley and alive with native species, this large stream is one of the few remaining unaltered and unspoiled in a natural state for its entire length.

Unnamed and remote, waterfalls plummet down the green wall of Oloku'i's east flank. With increasing rainfall, dormant water courses will spring to life and the number and volume will dramatically increase.

Contouring above the stream at times, the Wailau trail gradually ascends the valley. Vistas across the wide valley are frequent, and the sense of isolation in a seldom-visited wilderness increases.

Off Wailau Beach, the view down the coast is dominated by the great Oloku'i sea cliff.

From a vantage point a little above the base of Wailele Falls, the view extends west to Kalaupapa.
Hā'upu peak guarding the far entrance to Pelekunu Valley is the prominent landmark in the center.

Sun reflects off this sheer wall around the corner from Wailau. Hala trees are common in these areas, as in the foreground here, their exotic aerial roots providing needed stability in frequent steep and difficult coastal terrain.

Words like breathtaking and awesome still seem inadequate when pausing for awhile to admire a close-up view of the waterfalls pouring off this incredible sea cliff, the highest in the world.

As if the splendid cascade of Wailele Falls isn't enough, the sun will sometimes add a rainbow to the beauty of the scene as its rays catch the plume of spray shooting out from the pali.

79

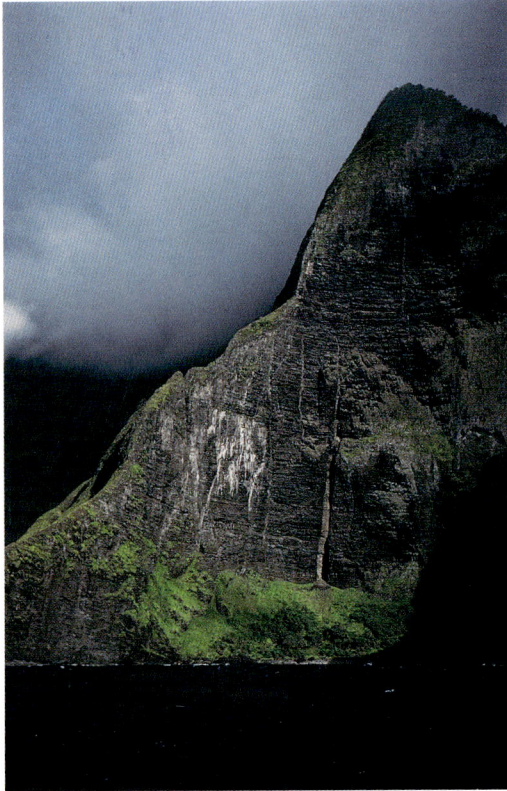

Under constant attack by waves at its base, the undermining process results in sea cliffs like this one looming over Kaholaiki Bay. Rainfall finishes the job of sculpturing the vertical face. Testifying to the ocean's power, waves rebound off these cliffs producing a chaotic, washing-machine effect familiar to the passing kayaker.

Pelekunu in Hawaiian means a place that has a moldy smell from lack of sunshine and prolonged rainfall. However along with showers come special moments like this double rainbow. (Photo by Rusty Lillico)

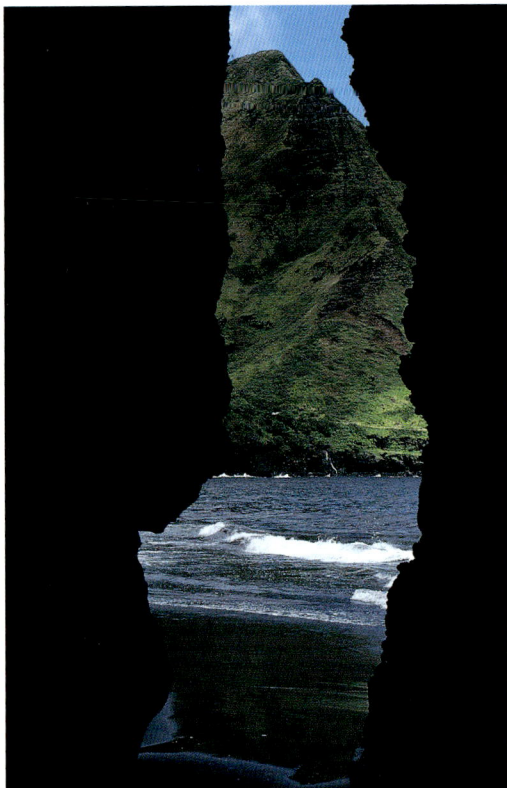

Pelekunu Valley's small, transient black-sand beach can be found near the mouth of Pelekunu Stream in the summer months. The remainder of the beach consists of boulders that rumble like huge bowling balls as the waves crash and recede. The valley itself, similar to Wailau but not as large or wide, is preserved now among the holdings of the Nature Conservancy on Moloka'i.

From Hā'upu Peak, the view eastward extends across Pelekunu Bay along the coast. Wailau's entrance can be seen in the middle distance.

A kayaker surveys the scene with 'Ōkala island dead ahead and the Kalaupapa peninsula in the distance.

This cave below Hā'upu Peak looks out on the ragged fang of Mokumanu, a 100-foot sea stack. The sea is often turbulent here and a challenge to paddling skills.

(Photo by Rusty Lillico)

Looking west over the relatively protected waters of Hāʻupu Bay toward the peninsula of Kalaupapa: Anapūhi Cave is located in the indentation in the spur near the center of the picture. The tiny buildings in the foreground are home for a Hawaiian family who have chosen to trade the conveniences of topside Molokaʻi for the solitude and vigors of life Hawaiian-style in this spectacular North coast location.

Shadows fall over the great chasm of the upper Wailau Valley. The rugged but very beautiful Wailau trail ascends steadily from the south shore to the edge of the precipice and then just above this point begins its plunge down the pali.

Oloku'i Peak (right center) at 4,602 feet is an isolated and pristine plateau that is free from the ravages of feral animals. The plateau's natural barriers of very steep cliffs and ridges have preserved one of the few remaining intact Hawaiian wet-forest ecosystems, and the area is a State Natural Area Reserve with a strict management plan intended to maintain its rare condition. Here clouds fill the upper reaches of Pelekunu Valley beyond the intervening ridge separating the heads of the two great valleys.

With less rainfall, the southern slope of the East Moloka'i shield volcano has much less erosion. This view extends downward along the route of the Wailau trail and out to the southwest between Maui on the left and Lāna'i.

In contrast to quiet East Moloka'i, across the deep blue waters of the Pailolo Channel on West Maui is another world of pineapple, sugar cane, golf courses and coastal tourist developments.

Sunset from the lower Wailau trail: Several of Moloka'i's many old fishponds are outlined on the darkened coast as the light fades from the sky over Lāna'i.

The Kaholo Pali, Lāna'i's highest sea cliff, is unusual because it is on the leeward side. Since the island lies in the rain shadow of Maui, the windward coast is sheltered from tradewind rainfall. On the opposite side, sea cliffs are formed by the assault of storm waves arriving from the southwest.

The Island Of
LĀNAʻI

LĀNAʻI

Hawaiʻi

Pu'u Pehe from the adjoining cliff: Now a prominent sea stack, it was once connected to the island by an arch. A walled structure with an upright stone is clearly visible on the summit.

The Island of Lāna'i

▲ ▲ ▲ ▲ ▲ ▲ ▲ ▲ ▲ ▲ ▲

Pu'u Pehe

Leaving the wind shadow of West Maui, Hōkūle'a eagerly surged forward as she began to encounter the large swells coming through the gap between Kaho'olawe and Lāna'i Ahead, now becoming hidden in the deepening shadows of late afternoon, was our Lāna'i destination, Mānele Bay. I was fortunate enough to be a Hōkūle'a crew member on this summer sail that was part of an educational program for outer island school children. It was a special thrill for me to be sailing on this famous, double-hulled Polynesian voyaging canoe that had already made several voyages to the South Pacific using ancient star navigational techniques. Relaxing in a prime location above the great steering paddles, I watched the canoe ride easily through four to six foot seas toward Mānele, now marked by the intermittent winking of a light on the breakwater. My thoughts drifted back to my last arrival at that harbor.

It was the last day of a kayak trip and we had spent the night at Kaunolū, the site of an ancient fishing village reputedly favored by Kamehameha I. Besides a number of house sites, walls, fishing shrines and a heiau, this place was noted for Kahekili's leap which was a distinct gap in the cliffs sixty feet above the water. Allegedly, for either sport or punishment, warriors once jumped off into the face of the prevailing trades, hoping to clear the twelve foot papa or reef shelf projecting out below. One Lāna'i old timer had told me on an earlier trip that if I jumped off and survived, he would make sure the name was changed to honor my leap. Standing there and looking down the first time, I quickly decided I liked the name just fine the way it was. The clear depths below the cliff were much better for fishing than jumping, and tasty pāpio had been on the previous night's menu.

We spent the morning exploring small caves and rocky inlets on the way to Hulopo'e Bay. Timing the surge to lift our kayaks up on a low shelf, we managed to land on a small islet and investigate some unusual endemic plants still thriving there in such an isolated ecosystem. A quick dive along the undersea walls revealed a wealth of nice coral, multihued algae, and sponges, in addition to a number of grazing pairs of brilliantly colored butterfly fish and a couple of big resident eels. Paddling on to the east, we began passing the broad crescent of beach at Hulopo'e. This picturesque bay where locals camped and picnicked had been given marine preservation status. Unfortunately, its future held plans for a large hotel and the usual golf course, so it was nice to be able to enjoy it without the harsh intrusion of concrete and condos.

As we made our way across the bay, I thought back to one of my first trips there. We had sailed over from O'ahu arriving late in the day, and as we maneuvered into position for anchoring that night, there was a noticeable clunk. After a quick assessment of the problem, the diagnosis of a missing propeller was made. Too late to look for it that evening, the following morning the search began in placid, calm water. Most of us were snorkelers on the lookout for anything suspicious. Visibility was excellent, and the ripples on the sandy bottom forty feet below were clearly visible. We began hearing some peculiar whistling sounds as though someone was trying to get our attention from the boat. Surfacing for a look, I saw that a group of dolphins had joined the hunt. Underwater again, the whistles and clicks became louder. Were we hearing these amazing mammals "talking story" in dolphinese or was it their sonar assessing the strangers nearby? It was much different than the strange moaning and groaning sounds I had heard from humpback

From Hokūle'a, Lāna'i falls into deep shadow under darkening skies. Pu'u Pehe stands out distinctly off the point.

whales. Shortly afterwards, the prop was spotted and retrieved. Perhaps our friends had just been trying to help us find it.

It was a pleasant memory, but on this day, there was no sign of activity as we left the bay and headed around the point. I decided to leave the others and take a few pictures further outside, using some partially submerged rocks for foreground framing. I had heard them described as the cathedral rocks, because of a series of underwater chambers and caverns where sunlight would stream down as though passing through stained glass windows in a Gothic cathedral. Although it was more the province of a scuba diver, I thought it would be fun to jump

over the side for a quick survey with mask and snorkel. But first came the photo session and I spent about a half hour trying different angles and settings. Some sooty terns added a little more interest to the pictures as they decided to stop by as if on cue.

Just after finishing the last shot on the roll, I reached around in back to pull out my fins and other gear. Turning back, I suddenly noticed something brown in the water ahead of me. A turtle more than likely, I thought. But with a more critical look, it dawned on me with a jolt that it was very definitely a fin and a large one at that. About a kayak's length in front of me and headed on a collision course was a very big shark. It was a stunning sight, and I sat there transfixed. I had seen sharks a few times before, mainly silhouetted on a backlit breaking wave when paddling out to go surfing. But never had I seen one from this perspective. It was like a Cousteau movie, I thought, as I noticed what looked like stripes on the shark's side. Then, a moment later, it seemed to veer off to the side, and it was gone. I stared at my shaking hands and shook my head at the unreality of it all. As scary as the whole experience was, I was struck with an appreciation of the way the shark so effortlessly disappeared with disdain for me while demonstrating total mastery of its environment. Hopefully, it was long gone at that point. As for my snorkeling gear, it would continue to lie unused at my feet on this occasion, needless to say.

Recovering from my unexpected excitement, I turned back in the direction of Pu'u Pehe, the large sea stack just around the corner from Hulopo'e. The whole area was once a cone whose seaward side had eroded, leaving a very scenic cove. On the eastern arm was an arch that had eventually collapsed resulting in an eighty foot pinnacle separated from a higher onshore cliff. This prominent coastal landmark had a very interesting background. The story as told by a Lāna'i native:

The girl Puupehe was the daughter of Uaua, a petty chief of the king of Maui. A native of Lana'i, Makakehau, captured her as the "joint prize of love and war." He was called Makakehau, Misty Eyes, because Puupehe's beauty had blinded him. His fear of losing such a beautiful girl led him to keep her in lonely places. One day, leaving her to prepare food in the sea cave of Malauea, he set out for the mountain spring of Pulou to fill his gourd with sweet water. Returning, he saw the front of a Kona storm approaching the coast. He rushed down the slope (three miles) to rescue his wife, but the waves had dashed into the cave, killing her. He recovered her body, which was wrapped in kapa for burial in the graveyard at the Kupapau of Manele. But that night he took the body to the top of the rock island; his friends were astonished to see him working on the grave there the next morning. He placed the last stone upon it, and then stretched his arms and wailed for Puupehe:

"Where are you, O Puupehe?
Are you in the cave of Malauea?
Shall I bring you sweet water?
The water of the mountain?
Shall I bring the *uwau* bird?
The *pala* fern and the *ohelo* berry?

You are baking the *honu* (turtle)
And the red, sweet hala.
Shall we dip in the gourd together?
The bird and the fish are bitter
And the mountain water is sour.
I shall drink it no more;
I shall drink it with Aipuhi,
The great shark of Manele."

Ceasing to wail, Makakehau leaped from the rock into the boiling surge at its base, his body was crushed in the breakers. The people who beheld the sad scene secured the corpse and buried it in the *kupapau* of Manele. (1)

Dr. Kenneth Emory, in 1921, explored the top of Pu'u Pehe, no small feat as the rock is vertical or overhanging on all sides. He found no evi-

dence of a burial site but only a platform measuring six feet wide, twenty one feet long, and three feet high with a stone sitting in an upright position near the center. He found a number of bird bones and speculated that perhaps the structure represented a bird hunter's shrine.(2) From the higher vantage point of the opposite cliff on shore, it is possible to look down on Pu'u Pehe and see this platform which stands in the center of the island and appears to be in good condition.

As far as actually seeing for yourself, a helicopter seems to offer the best possibility. However, as I paddled closer, I saw a figure spread-eagled on the rock about halfway up. It was Bob, our intrepid botanist, who didn't discourage easily and was intent on finding Dr. Emory's route to the summit. His wife, who was watching nearby, decided she'd seen enough and began to paddle away. Shaking her head, she said "I'm leaving. I don't want to watch anymore." Fortunately, Bob decided he was in a dead-end position and began to reverse course with a careful descent. There would be no new breakthroughs in the mystery of Pu'u Pehe from our group. The main thing though, was to avoid taking any casualties at this late stage in a great trip, and so the rest of the way back to Mānele passed all too quickly.

My reminiscing completed, darkness was almost upon us as Hōkūle'a glided into the calm, protected water of the harbor. Now this is the best way to visit the islands of Hawai'i, I thought. High above, Hōkūle'a's namesake star was now visible. What of Pu'upehe? Did Lāna'i tradition have a star for her up there somewhere? Did I happen to run into Aipuhi, the great shark of Mānele that day? Lāna'i known primarily to tourists as the Pineapple Isle, has its share of mysteries and legends as part of a rich, cultural heritage.

(1) Emory, Kenneth P. : The Island of Lana'i.
Bulletin #12, page 15. Bishop Museum Press, 1924
(2) Ibid. page 72

For those who are fascinated by
offshore islets and sea stacks,
Nānāloa gets a five-star rating.
Replete with legend and very scenic,
this group of striking pinnacles is a
well-recognized feature of the southwestern Lānaʻi coast. Offering good
snorkeling, fishing and even a cave
to explore, a visit here is a highlight
Lānaʻi experience.

(Photos by Ann Fielding.)

Roaring tradewinds funneling through the Kalohi Channel between Lāna'i and Moloka'i have contributed to the demise of many vessels whose remains litter the 8-mile stretch of northern coast aptly named Shipwreck Beach.

Although an occasional treasure like a glass ball can still turn up, the majority of the finds are driftwood along with a vast assortment of planks, timbers, and other pieces of once-proud ships (left). Below: Of the numerous shipwrecks, this ship is one of two still intact and visible off the beach.

Lāna'i's best petroglyphs are found on boulder sites like this one near the eastern end of Shipwreck Beach.

Even though accessible by 4-wheel drive vehicles, these long stretches of windy, white-sand beach backed by low sand dunes see few visitors except for occasional fishermen and beachcombers (below).

A typical Lāna'i coastal campsite: Low eroded bluffs, a small boulder beach, and probably fresh fish for dinner.

A small fleet of kayakers paddle beneath the dry, barren Kahalo Pali. This section has a shallow, black-sand beach which is good for a stop along the way for exploring but not for camping.

A cliff near Kaunolū is profiled against an early evening sky as a placid sea reflects some of sunset's palette of color.

Waves crash into the tidepool shelf below Kaunolū as brisk mid-day winds blow along the coast.

Kaunolū, an ancient fishing village favored by the Kamehamehas, is another highlight on a kayak tour of Lāna'i. Although the area can be reached by a rough, bumpy 4-wheel drive road, a visit by kayak is certainly more comfortable unless a rough sea makes landing difficult. Fishing is still very good, and the many platforms, walls, and a heiau at this National Historic Landmark are well preserved.

From a vantage point on the cliffs above, Kaunolū's small bay is located in the center of the picture with the navigational light on the white tower on the point beyond. Ma'o (a native cotton related to hibiscus with large yellow flowers) and other Hawaiian coastal plants can be found on these dry slopes.

Afternoon shadows fill West Maui's deep valleys in this view across Hōkūle'a's stern. Due to the less resistant rock, the smaller and older of Maui's two volcanos exhibits a considerable degree of stream dissection on this drier, southwestern slope.

The Island Of
MAUI

MAUI

Hawai'i

Beautiful Waimoku Falls, above Seven Pools Park in Kīpahulu, comes into view through dense stream-side vegetation. The scenic trail climbs above 'Ohe'o stream through sunny pasture land and a dark, creaking bamboo forest.

The Island of Maui

▲ ▲ ▲ ▲ ▲ ▲ ▲ ▲ ▲ ▲ ▲

Maui Dawn

The throbbing beat of an approaching helicopter shattered the stillness of a grey Maui dawn. The chopper roared angrily overhead and then disappeared into the dark curtain of a rain squall in the distance. There were several more in quick succession, and I was jolted out of the fog of early morning sleep. Shaking off the usual Vietnam memories at the sound, I realized that these choppers were on a special sightseeing mission on this very unique morning. It was Eclipse Day 1991, and we were perfectly positioned to witness one of nature's most spectacular shows.

However, watching the rain drip down outside the entrance to our cave on this remote section of southeastern Maui coastline, it began to appear that the weather gods were in the process of dealing a death blow to months of careful planning. Our campsite had been reached by two hours of paddling, and it was only accessible from the sea as 60 to 80 foot cliffs of basaltic lava rose above us. There was a sizable, picturesque tidepool protected by a rough, rocky, outer sea-wall and on the inside was a small, black-sand beach. Near the junction of this outer barrier with the main cliff, was an underwater tunnel which provided a connection between the ocean and an inner separate well-like chamber. Periodically, an extra large swell would surge through, creating a small waterfall as this chamber overflowed into the pool. The enclosed, isolated pool seemed to have its own ecosystem, and a quick survey with mask and snorkel revealed an abundance of reef fish and healthy coral. Large 'opihi appeared to be dying of old age on the rocks—a sure sign of very few visitors. The whole setting was an ideal site for kayakers as the only nearby landing possibility was a small, relatively protected boulder-strewn cove on an otherwise rugged and unfriendly coastline.

At present, instead of the glorious sunrise we had anticipated, there was a strange and somber grey cast to the surroundings as the sky began to darken. The day before, late in the afternoon, we had been treated to a brilliant 180 degree rainbow after a passing rain squall. In this area of minimal annual rainfall, we had half-jokingly speculated about the possibility of bad weather on the big morning. As totality approached, there was no question now that the concern we had lightly dismissed was becoming a reality.

There was an eerie stillness, and a few sea birds flew past, convinced somehow that it was time to head for home. One more large helicopter landed on the ridge above the bay opposite us. Its passengers, their yellow, foul-weather gear distinct against the gloom, began the apparently futile exercise of setting up tripods and telescopes. Shortly, even without a watch, we knew the moment was at hand. We were not only submerged in more darkness, but it became distinctly cooler. A light breeze passed over as the wind appeared to shift slightly. The dragon had indeed swallowed the sun, and it was an awe-inspiring feeling in spite of the disappointing

A conglomerate cliff of lava debris near Kaʻīlio Point frames the rough, lava coastline looking back in the direction of Kaupō.

view. The impact in ancient times must have been incredible, and even in our sophisticated high-tech age, there was a definite sense of relief when light and warmth began to return to the earth.

Soon, as if to reassure us that all was back to normal, the sun broke through the cloud cover for the first time. With the use of our special Mylar filters, we could gaze at the sun and see that it was still suffering from a forty percent bite. We sat there savoring the whole experience. After all, we had just been part of something that last occurred in Hawai'i a mere 141 years ago and would not happen again here until the year 2106!

Life began to return to our tidepool campsite as the wind began to pick up and send waves crashing into the outer barrier. After enjoying our stay a few more hours, we packed up the kayak and paddled out into the jet-stream of wind and swells pushing us down to our take-out destination. Speeding past the point, we caught a last glimpse of this remarkable place as the pool and all its special features blended into a view of

jumbled rock formations and crashing waves. On this island where tourists lounge around hotel pools, we had been fortunate enough to experience an extraordinary event in a very unique location. Thank you, Maui!

Wet rocks glisten on the shore of Wailua Valley near Hana. Although overgrown with dense brush and numerous coconut palms, the extensive taro terraces that once existed in this small valley are still distinguishable.

From the welcome shelter of a convenient cave, a rainbow brightens the grey sky as unexpected rain showers blow in from the sea on the afternoon before the eclipse.

105

A very picturesque pool and waterfall are hidden away just above the rocky shore in the 'Ula'ino area. On the way, a visit to massive Pi'ilanihale Heiau, the largest heiau in Hawai'i, is very worthwhile.

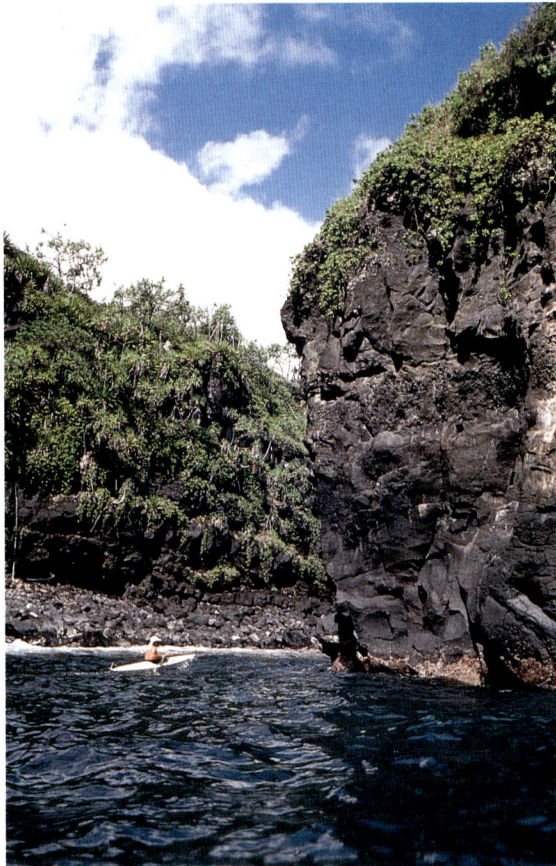

The verdant but rough coastline in the Hana region is well-suited to exploration by kayak.

(Photo by Ann Fielding)

Hala or pandanus trees are silhouetted hanging out over the bluff above. These very adaptive trees, originally from Asia, have leaves and fruits which have a multitude of uses for Polynesian people.

Camping out features a mouth-watering meal Hawaiian-style, including fish and 'opihi stew.

107

(Preceding pages)
Mountains to the sea:
A spectacular vista of wild and
remote Kīpahulu Valley from
high on the rim of Haleakalā.

110

Just after dawn, early morning's magic light transforms a stark, rocky slope with a golden glow as clouds are tinged with pink.

Backpackers enter the unique and strange, multihued moonscape world of western Haleakalā crater along the Sliding Sands trail. Here clouds begin to fill the Koolau Gap, one of the two great eroded breaks in the crater wall.

111

The Park Service's Palikū cabin is a welcome sight to backpackers after a 9-1/2 mile hike from the Sliding Sands trailhead. Here in the windward eastern end of the crater, rainfall is frequent and the result is a dramatic change in the surroundings compared to the dry, barren terrain of the western crater. Experiencing a clear day at Palikū is one of Hawaii's very special moments, and the views from the rim above and down Kaupō Gap are magnificent.

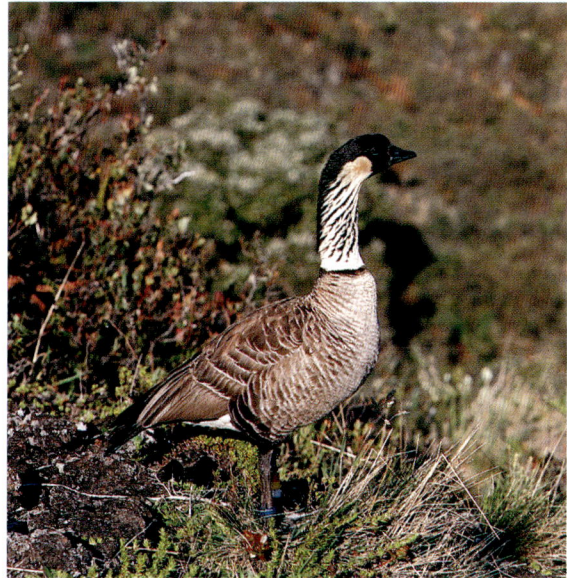

Nēnē, the native Hawaiian goose (*Nesochen sandvicensis*), are often seen around Palikū. An endangered species and also Hawaii's State Bird, bands are visible on this bird but not its peculiar feet which have evolved to lose most of the webbing.

Having a reservation for the Palikū cabin is a real luxurious feeling, but with a good tent, camping in this beautiful location can be equally enjoyable.

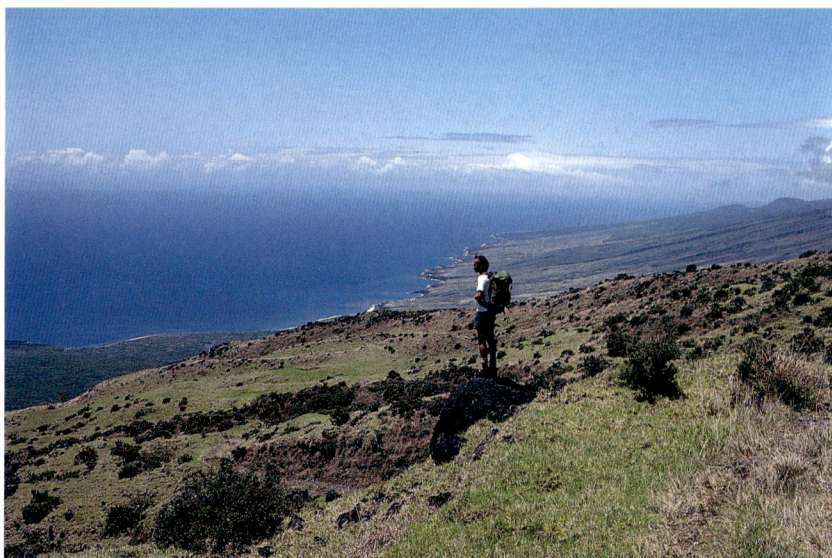

The trail out Kaupō Gap descends over 6,000-feet and results in wobbly knees. Leaving behind the often mist-shrouded upper portion of the trail, thoughts of just a short uphill break from the relentless downhill grind can be eased by the expansive views down to the distant ocean.

The lush interior of 'Īao Valley is a world of dense vegetation where the most feasible route is often following one of the streams upward toward the headwall of the caldera. Hawaiians once used a route from 'Īao over to Olowalu Valley on the western side, but the journey is hazardous and very difficult today.

The main branches of 'Īao stream are clear with beautiful inviting pools and tantalizing smaller side-streams that tumble down from cool, fern-shrouded grottoes. Large 'ēkaha or bird's nest ferns are often seen as in the branches of this kukui tree.

Kahakuloa Head or Pu'u Koa'e is a well-known landmark on the north coast of West Maui. A scramble up to the 636-foot summit reveals this view looking across Kahakuloa Bay along the low sea cliffs toward East Moloka'i.

Day's end on West Maui: The sun begins to sink below a layer of clouds. Moloka'i is a golden shadow in the background.

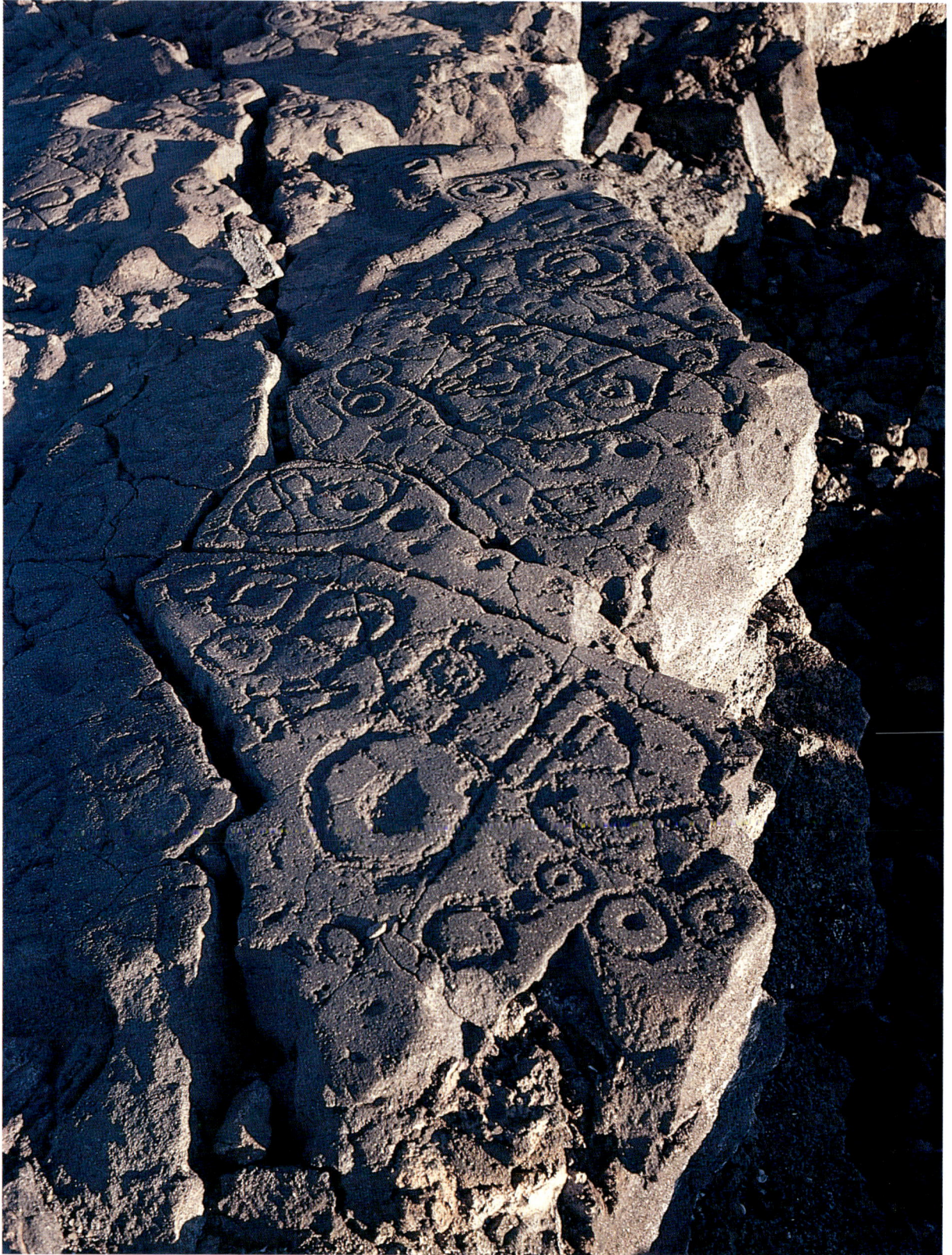

Petroglyphs are found in greater number and concentration on the Big Island than anywhere else in the islands. The mystery and questions that surround many of them are part of the special awareness of the past that is part of a visit to this largest, youngest, and most diverse island of the Hawaiian chain.

The Island Of

HAWAIʻI

HAWAIʻI

Hawaiʻi

As the harsh, lava coastal landscape is softened by late afternoon light, small waves break on a lonely, coral rubble beach south of Miloli'i in South Kona.

The Island of Hawai'i

▲ ▲ ▲ ▲ ▲ ▲ ▲ ▲ ▲ ▲ ▲

South Kona

I was walking along an old Hawaiian trail through a tortured lava flow. Standing out in stark contrast to the barren landscape, large smooth stones from the sea marked the way. I decided to take a short detour to investigate a particularly striking formation of twisted pāhoehoe. It offered some interesting photographic possibilities, but as I positioned myself for the shot, I accidentally dropped my lens cap down into a small hollow. I found it wedged in a pile of lava rubble at the base of a low wall. Reaching down to retrieve the cap, I felt a curious rush of cool air. It seemed to be coming through the wall somehow. Taking a closer look, I noticed a small opening. I pulled away a few of the rocks, and suddenly realized I was staring into the entrance of some kind of lava tube.

Cautiously, I climbed through the ragged hole I had created. Once inside, crouching slightly, I took a few tentative steps forward. The tube stretched away ahead of me. It sloped a little downhill into the darkness, but then at the far end, it seemed to get lighter again. As if drawn by an irresistible, magnetic force, I stumbled down the passageway which was quite clear of any rocky debris. Halfway along, there was an area where the ceiling became lower and the tunnel narrowed. Fighting off a panicky feeling of being trapped and encouraged by another light rush of cooler air, I squeezed past this section. A short distance further, I found myself standing in a large chamber. Ahead, the cave was partially blocked by large rocks; around the corner, I could hear the muffled sound of crashing waves. The high-arched ceiling

had no discernible opening in the roof, which was at least twenty feet above me. But my gaze was riveted on a ledge a little above me on the right. For there was a large canoe, its wood shining dully in the subdued light. Alongside were several large calabashes and some small stone images. My heart pounding in amazement, I climbed carefully up alongside and peered into the canoe. Two skeletons lay inside, each covered partially by what must have been the fibrous remains of tapa cloth. The nearest figure had shriveled, mummified skin on its legs with some distinguishable elaborate tatooing. Its sightless eyes stared back accusingly at me as I stepped back and almost tripped over several paddles lying next to the canoe. Who were they? How did they get the canoe inside? Questions raced through my mind as I tried to assimilate the incredible sight before me.

Hearing the sound of waves, I decided to explore the front of the chamber. As I reached the obstructing rocks and began to pick my way around them, I was unexpectedly and without warning struck by a wall of water. At the same time, above me came a drenching downpour. Somehow, I had fallen down and in trying to sit up, I struck my head on some kind of plank. Or was it a paddle? My senses reeled as I suddenly realized that I was not in a burial chamber at all but lying on a beach underneath a leaky tarp spread over two paddles and the 'iakos of an outrigger canoe.

It was all an unbelievable dream! But it was so vividly real, I thought, as I tried to get my bearings. I looked at my wife Olga who was huddled in the

The amazing hōlua slide at Puʻu Hinahina: Before cheering spectators, aliʻi once ran down this runway before jumping on their sleds at the top of the ramp.

corner of our makeshift shelter taking advantage of the only semi-dry area. "Hey, it's not supposed to rain like this around here," I said "I know," she replied miserably, "but we sure are getting a good soaking." We were camped on a beach south of Miloliʻi on the South Kona coast in an area that was not known for such rainfall. Still trying to shake myself back to reality, I told her about my dream as I tried to do something about our very porous roof. It was 4:00 A.M. and outside there were relentless sheets of rain blowing in off the ocean.

We were part of a Hawaii Bound group that had taken off from Miloliʻi three days before for an outrigger canoe trip. Up to now, we had been having a great time and had been treated to good weather, relatively calm seas, and comfortable campsites. This region was seldom visited except by an occasional fisherman, and all around us we

had seen reminders that this coast was once well-populated. It was a lonely place now, but it had a desolate, haunting beauty. In the evening, especially, listening to the creaking branches as wind blew through the kiawe trees, you could easily imagine the presence of those who once inhabited this region. As in my dream, we had walked across desolate lava flows on old Hawaiian trails. From time to time, even a considerable distance from shore, you could hear the hissing and moaning sound of air rushing through a hidden lava tube. It seemed as though in some places the area was honeycombed with these tubes. People have speculated that Kamehameha the Great even lay buried somewhere along this storied coast. Could he be in such a place? It was a time for thoughts of Hawaiian legends and stories that always became much more believable on Big Island visits.

Our camp the previous night had been on a beach close to an old Hawaiian village site. There was a heiau partially overgrown with kiawe and brush as well as a number of walls and house site platforms. We swam in the refreshingly cool water of a small spring located in a shady spot in the midst of rough, rocky terrain not too far from the sea. There was a well with brackish water where we spent some time clearing out the black mud and debris choking the surface. A stone trail led off in the direction of the cloud-shrouded forests on the upper slopes far above us. Would we see the fabled marchers of the night of Hawaiian legends? (1) If it were ever to happen, this mysterious and mournful location certainly would seem to be a likely place.

Also, standing out in stark contrast to the disorder of the rugged lava landscape was a very well-preserved hōlua slide looking like a primitive launching pad for some sort of alien spacecraft. This ancient sport favored especially among the ali'i was conducted using narrow sleds on a long incline either on a natural slope, or as in this case, a specially constructed ramp. It was paved on the surface with well-fitting smooth stones on which had once been placed a layer of grass on top of packed earth. After bets had been placed, the objective was to ride the sled, on runners lubricated with kukui nut oil, down the incline and out onto the level area at the end of the course with the greatest distance travelled determining the winner.(2) I had climbed to the top and tried to imagine the scene. It was amazing how well this particular slide had survived the years. I wondered how old it was as I looked down over its carefully constructed slope as the late afternoon Kona sun began to sink into the shimmering sea. As Olga had mentioned to me, there was a feeling that we were almost trespassing in an area that wasn't meant to be disturbed.

The following day, we had paddled north to land on a fine, broad grey-sand beach fronting Okoe Bay. In the evening, we had built a large fire on the beach after dinner, as it was our last night. Some of the more adventurous of the group had decided on a night dive to celebrate the occasion. We had only two lights to share among six people, and we quickly became interested in togetherness as we swam out in the inky black water. It was especially spooky on this dark night devoid of moon or stars. As usual, the underwater world on the reef was fascinating, but it was a relief to surface and still see the reassuring beacon of our fire on the shore. Earlier, there had been a few light sprinkles, so before turning in for the night we had casually rigged up our shelter, not really expecting much need for protection in this generally dry area.

Now as the sky began to lighten with the first signs of the coming of dawn, we could see nothing but curtains of rain blowing across wind-whipped grey swells in the bay. Deciding we might as well be out paddling instead of standing around on the beach getting soaked, we quickly packed the canoes and headed for Miloli'i. In a short time, conditions began to improve and amazingly, in another hour and a half things were almost back to normal. Perhaps we had offended Madame Pele in some way, and now she had relented and dismissed the storm. By the time we reached Miloli'i, it had turned out to be a beautiful, classic Kona day with no hint of bad weather remaining. Watching some local youngsters nonchalantly ride waves through a tight gap in the offshore rocks, we ate lunch in the sunshine and reflected on the many highs of our South Kona adventure.

Returning from a walk to the small store, I found Olga enjoying the view from the shade of an ironwood tree.

"Hey, guess what?" I said.

"Don't tell me," she said, making a face, "the pick-ups are going to be late."

"Nope, nothing like that," I laughed. "The word from the locals is that the little cloud we were under was the worst storm to hit that area in the last thirty years!"

Was it a parting shot or a special blessing?

This quiet shoreline was once populated by Hawaiians living in small fishing villages. Nearby are brackish water springs and a large heiau overgrown now with kiawe.

Either way it punctuated our visit to South Kona with an exciting finish, and we bounced up the road in a time-warp return to modern Hawai'i with some very special memories.

(1) Beckwith, Martha: Hawaiian Mythology. University of Hawaii Press, 1970, page 164.
".....Family ties in the afterworld remain unbroken, and all Hawaiians believe in the power of spirits to return to

the scenes they knew on earth in the form in which they appeared while they were alive. Especially this is true of the processions of gods and spirits who come on certain sacred nights to visit the sacred places, or to welcome a dying relative and conduct him to the 'aumakua world. "Marchers of the night" (Huaka'i or "spirit ranks" (Oi'o) they are called.

(2) Malo, David: Hawaiian Antiquities. Bishop Museum Press. 1951, pages 224-225.

Wandering along these isolated shores brings the enjoyment of lots of solitude, clear skies, and a panoramic vista of the great bulk of Mauna Loa above.

From Ohepuupuu, a small 100-foot benchmark hill in a sea of ʻāʻa lava, a telephoto view gives a different perspective on Kapuʻa Bay with Hualalai looming in the background.

A wave breaks offshore near Kapuʻa Bay in this view north toward Okoe Bay and Hanamalo Point.

Kiawe and Kona orange sky (left).

South Kona Sunset...

Goodby for today: The sun slips beneath the waves (left).

*Full moon and lava:
With a little imagina-
tion, ghostly shapes
come to life (right).*

...and Moon

*Dawn with a
fading moon
(left).*

*Brilliant full moon
with clouds
(right).*

125

Stepping-stone trails criss-cross rough 'ā'a lava flows and provide convenient routes through inhospitable terrain. Some have very large, waterworn stones (pa'alā) and lead upward toward the mountains as well as along the coast..

Views from inside and outside a South Kona sea cave/lava tube: Are some yet to be explored?

Skirting Kamā'ohe Bay, a trail heads south to Niu'ou, once known for a large coconut grove but now a lonely place with habitation sites hidden by brush and large kiawe trees.

The Kona Coast is favored by divers because of good visibility and abundant marine life on healthy reefs. Here a snorkeler appears to hang suspended above the reef.

Yellow tangs dart in and out of coral crevices in sunny and clear Kona waters.

Early morning sun slants across a beach south of Ho'okena. The flank of Mauna Loa with its classic shield volcano profile slopes gradually down to the sea in the background.

With a little imagination, this well-defined lava flow transforms into a fiery, red-hot river of molten lava. It actually occurred in 1950, making it barely cooled from a geological time standpoint.

A long stretch of black sand beach extends for 2 miles along the shore of Kīholo Bay. Near here, Kamehameha I constructed a very large fish pond which was subsequently destroyed by the lava flow of 1859 from Mauna Loa. Kohala Mountain, with its large cinder cones visible even from a distance, is in the background.

Between Ka'ūpūlehu and Kīholo, a section of shoreline was spared by the 1801 Hualālai lava flow which surrounds it on both the north and south. Storm surf washes sand and coral debris over the low sea cliffs, creating a number of shallow rock basins that accumulate salt after the water evaporates.

With clouds hanging over Hualālai, the spacious expanse of the Big Island can be appreciated in this panoramic view from the north end of Kīholo Bay.

Canoes with crab-claw sails like these were once a common sight in Kīholo Bay. Patterned after this design, these same sails have served Hōkūle'a well in her Pacific voyages.

The aquamarine water of the Kīholo lagoon, with its coconut trees, is a striking coastal landmark. Green sea turtles frequent this sheltered location, and it has been proposed as a marine sanctuary for these protected animals.

This natural rock garden with its symmetrical rock placement and fine textured black sand appear to have been the work of a Japanese master (above).

Speculation is that these paddle-men may be symbolic of canoe paddlers in general and not representative of any kind of dance or competition (right).

Pele's intriguing designs are to be found on a walk through an area of pāhoehoe lava (below).

Running straight across the lava, this inland trail, the Ala Loa, was constructed around 1871 for the purpose of driving cattle between Kīholo and Kawaihae. A seven-mile, well-preserved section between the Mauna Lani Hotel and Kīholo has been designated for protection on the Hawaii Register of Historic Places.

Looking down on Waimanu Beach from the Waimanu Trail: Crossing over the heads of nine smaller valleys, the 11-mile journey from Waipi'o is nearly over at this point. Once used by mule trains to bring taro and other produce out of the valley, this memorable route is used now by backpackers and pig hunters. Camping is by permit only in order to help protect and preserve this wilderness valley.

Before beginning a 1,100-foot descent to the valley floor, the trail provides a view to the northwest across the bay and the Waimanu sea cliff. Further along the base of the cliff is Laupāhoehoe Nui, a shallow peninsula which was terraced and farmed.

The beach at Waimanu is mostly boulders, but in the summer, black sand accumulates at the western end. It is an enjoyable place for a refreshing swim especially after a long hike, and bodysurfing can be good in waves breaking over a sand bar.

135

Rain showers blow through Honokāne Nui Valley as seen from its eastern rim. Like several other North Kohala valleys, it was also extensively cultivated. However, with the building of the Kohala Ditch trail in 1901 to divert water for sugar, adequate irrigation became more difficult, taro farming diminished, and eventually agriculture in the valley was abandoned.

Waipi'o Valley from the Waimanu trail: The beauty of Waipi'o has been celebrated in song and legend, and the extensive cultivation of the wide valley was unequalled on the island. The steep 4-wheel drive road leading down into the valley stands out distinctly on the opposite side.

In this view from the ridge to the west, Honokāne Nui stream runs into the ocean past a grove of ironwoods. Much of the lower valley has been overrun by aggressive introduced vegetation, and the walls and the terraces of the past are hard to find (right).

(Preceding pages) Idyllic appearing Waimanu stream winds through the valley to reach the sea just past this point. Up until the end of the nineteenth century, Hawaiians grew taro extensively in this beautiful valley now taken over by alien grasses and bulrushes.

Glossary

'a'ā Rough, broken, and chunky lava.

'ama'u All species of endemic genus of ferns (*Sadleria spp.*).

'aumakua Family or personal god.

banana poka Pernicious introduced vine (*Passiflora mollisima*).

calabash Bowl made from various woods or a gourd.

clidemia hirta One of the worst of alien plants in O'ahu. Commonly found in O'ahu rain forests, now invading other islands.

hāpu'u Endemic tree fern (*Cibotium spp.*).

heiau Pre-Christian place of worship. Some were elaborately constructed stone platforms while others were simple earth terraces.

Hōkūle'a Sixty-foot double hulled Polynesian voyaging canoe. First sailed to Tahiti in 1976 using ancient star navigational methods. Named after zenith star for Hawaii, Arcturus in the constellation Böotes.

hōlua Sled with runners about six inches wide and twelve feet long. Runners were made of māmane or uhiuhi wood.

'ie'ie Endemic woody climber (*Freycinetia arborea*). Found commonly in elevations of over 1,500 feet .

'i'iwi One of native honeycreepers. Scarlet feathers used for cloaks and featherwork. Still present in significant numbers on the Big Island and on Maui.

ironwood Lowland or dry forest tree. Hardy and wind resistant. Native of Australia *(Casurarina equisetifolia)*.

'iako Outrigger canoe boom.

kanawao Common shrub of wet higher elevation areas with large, oval and toothed leaves (*Broussaisia arguta*). An old belief was that eating the fruit increased fecundity.

kiawe The algaroba tree (*Prosopis pallida*) from Tropical America. Common in dry coastal areas.

koa Largest of endemic forest trees (*Acacia koa*) with light grey bark and crescent-shaped leaves. Fine red wood used formerly for canoes, surfboards, and calabashes; now used for furniture, interiors, and ukuleles.

koa'e-kea White-tailed tropic birds (*Phaethon lepturus dorothea*) which inhabits cliffs of high islands.

Ko'olau Literally windward. Mountain range running north and south and dividing windward from central O'ahu.

kukui Candlenut tree *(Aleurites moluccana)*. Multiple uses for nuts whose oily kernels were used as lights and as a source of oil for lubrication or rubbing; also for ornamental purposes when polished. Soft wood used for canoes. Gum from bark for painting tapa. Also black dye from nut coats and roots.

Glossary (continued)

lapalapa   Endemic mountain tree *(Cheirodendron spp.)* with delicate appearing leaves that flutter in the wind.

loulu   Endemic fan palm *(Pritchardia* spp.).

kupapaʻu   Cemetery.

ʻōhelo   Small endemic shrub *(Vaccinium reticulatum)* in cranberry family. Red or yellow berries edible raw or cooked in sauce.

ʻōhiʻa   Dominant Hawaiian rain forest tree *(Metrosideros polymorpha)*

ʻopihi   Any of species of edible limpet.

pāhoehoe. Smooth unbroken type of lava.

pala   Endemic fern *(Marattia douglasii).* Edible and used also for medicinal purposes. For heiau ceremonies.

pali   Cliff or precipice.

papa   Flat surface such as reef flat.

pāpio   Young growth stage of ulua or jack.

Pele   Volcano goddess.

pūhi   Any eel.

sooty tern   Slender graceful seabird with black upperparts. Ewaʻewa in Hawaiian: "to make uncomfortable from incessant screeching."

tapa (kapa)   Cloth made from bark of wauke or paper mulberry tree.

ua liʻl liʻl   Fine misty rain.

ʻuki   Coarse native sedges.

ʻuwaʻu   Petrel or type of seabird.

140

Bibliography

A. General

Beckwith, Martha: Hawaiian Mythology. University of Hawaii Press, 1970.

Daws, Gavan: Shoal of Time. Macmillan, 1968. Reprint: University of Hawaii Press, 1974.

Ibid, Hawaii: Islands of Life. Signature Publishing, 1988.

Elbert, Samuel and Mahoe, Noelani: Na Mele o Hawaii Nei. University of Hawaii Press, 1970.

Chisholm, Craig: Hawaiian Hiking Trails, Fernglen Press.

Dept. of Geography. Atlas of Hawaii: University of Hawaii. University of Hawaii Press, 1983.

II, John Papa: Fragments of Hawaiian History, Bishop Museum Press, 1959.

Kamakau, Samuel: Ka Po'e Kahiko, the People of Old. Bishop Museum Special Publication No.51, 1964.

Ibid, Ruling Chiefs of Hawaii. Kamehameha Schools, 1961.

Kirch, Patrick: Feathered Gods and Fishhooks: An Introduction to Hawaiian Archaeology and Prehistory. University of Hawaii Press, 1985.

Malo, David: Hawaiian Antiquities. Bishop Museum Press, 1971.

Pukui, Mary Kawena and Elbert, Samuel: Hawaiian Dictionary. University of Hawaii Press, 1986.

Ibid, Haety, M. E.W. and Lee, Catherine A.: Nana i ke Kumu. Volumes I and II, Queen Liliuokalani Children's Center.

Ibid and Mookini, Esther: Place Names of Hawaii. University of Hawaii Press, 1974.

Rice, William Hyde: Hawaiian Legends. Bishop Museum Special Publication No.63, 1977.

Smith, Robert: Hiking Hawaii. Wilderness Press, 1977.

Sutherland, Audrey: Paddling Hawai'i. The Mountaineers, 1988.

Scott, Edward B.: The Saga of the Sandwich I Islands. Sierra-Tahoe Publishing, 1968.

B. Natural History

Fielding, Ann and Robinson, Edward: An Underwater Guide to Hawaii. University of Hawaii Press, 1987.

Harrison, Craig S.: Seabirds of Hawaii. Cornell University Press, 1990.

Hawaii's Birds. Hawaiian Audubon Society, 1986

Kaufman, Gregory D. and Forestel, Paul H.: Hawaiian Humpback Whales. Pacific Whale Foundation Press, 1986.

Kepler, Angela K.: Hawaiian Heritage Plants. Oriental Publishing, 1984.

Kimura, Bert Y. and Nagata, Kenneth M.: Hawaii's Vanishing Flora. Oriental Publishing, 1980.

Kyselka, Will and Lanterman, Ray: North Star to Southern Cross. University of Hawaii Press, 1976.

Macdonald, Gordon, Abbot, Agatha, and Peterson, Frank L: Volcanoes in the Sea, University of Hawaii Press, 1983.

Neal, Marie C.: In Gardens of Hawaii. Bishop Museum Press, 1965.

Pratt, Douglas and Bruner, Philip L.: Field Guide to Birds of Hawaii and the Tropical Pacific. Princeton University Press, 1987.

Sohner, S. H. and Gustafson, R.: Plants and Flowers of Hawaii. University of Hawaii Press, 1987.

Titcomb, Margaret: Native Use of Fish in Hawaii. University of Hawaii Press, 1965.

C. O'ahu

Clark, John R.K.: The Beaches of O'ahu. University of Hawaii Press, 1976.

Macdonald, Gordon A. and Kyselka, W.: Anatomy of an Island: A Geological History of O'ahu. Bishop Museum Press, 1967.

McAlister, J.: Archaeology of O'ahu. Bishop Museum Press, 1933.

Bibliography (continued)

Meyen, Dr. F.J.F.: A Botanist's Visit to O'ahu in 1931. Press Pacifica Ltd. 1981.

Paki, Pilahi: Legends of Hawaii. O'ahu Yesterday. Victoria Publications, 1972.

Sterling, Elspeth and Summers, Catherine: The Sites of O'ahu. Bishop Museum Press, 1962 .

D. Kaua'i

Bennett, Wendell Clark: Archaeology of Kaua'i. Bishop Museum Bulletin No.30, 1931.

Armitage, George and Judd, Henry: Ghost Dogs and other Hawaiian Legends. Advertiser Publisher Co., 1944.

Clark, John R.K.: The Beaches of Kaua'i. University of Hawaii Press, 1988.

Durkin, Pat: The Kaua'i Guide to Beaches, Water Activities, and Safety. Magic Fishes Press, 1988.

Gilman, G.D.: "Journal of a Canoe Voyage along the Kaua'i Palis made in 1845." Hawaiian Historical Society Papers, No.14, 1908.

Thurston, Lorrin P.: The Kingdom of Nualolo. Honolulu Advertiser, July 20, 1922.

Valier, Kathy: On the Na Pali Coast. University of Hawaii Press, 1988.

Yent, Martha: "Archaeological Mapping: Nualolo Aina, Na Pali Coast, Kaua'i," State of Hawaii, DLNR, Div. of State Parks, Honolulu, 1983.

E. Moloka'i

Bushnell, O. A.: Moloka'i. The World Publishing Co., 1983.

Clark, John R.K.: The Beaches of Maui County. University of Hawaii Press, 1980.

Cooke III, Richard A.: Molokai: An Island in Time. Beyond Words Publishing, 1984.

Daws, Gavan: Holy Man: Father Damien of Moloka'i. Harper and Row, 1973.

Summers, Catherine C.: Moloka'i: A Site Survey. Bishop Museum Press, 1974.

Sutherland, Audrey: Paddling My Own Canoe. University of Hawaii Press, 1978.

F. Lāna'i

Emory, Kenneth: The Island of Lanai. Bishop Museum Bulletin No.12, 1924.

Finney, Ben R.: Hokule'a: The Way to Tahiti. Dodd, Mead, and Co., 1979.

Kyselka, Will: An Ocean in Mind. University of Hawaii Press, 1987.

Tabrah, Ruth: Lanai, Island Heritage Press, 1976.

G. Maui

Kepler, C.B. and Kepler, A.K.: Haleakala: A Guide to the Mountain. Mutual Publishing, 1988.

Sterling, Elspeth: "The Sites of Maui County" 14 vol. Bishop Museum Department of Archaeology. Unpublished manuscript.

Wenkam, Robert: Maui: The Last Hawaiian Place. Friends of the Earth, 1970.

H. Hawai'i

Bushnell,O.A.: The Return of Lono. Little, Brown and Co., 1956. Reprint: University of Hawaii Press, 1971.

Clark, John R. K.: The Beaches of the Big Island. University of Hawaii Press, 1985.

Ellis, William: Journal of William Ellis. Charles Tuttle, 1979.

Grant, Glen: Hawaii: The Big Island. Mutual and Signature Publishing, 1988.

Tregakis, Richard: The Warrior King. Hawaii's Kamehameha the Great. Falmouth Press, 1973.